WRECKS
&
REPUTATIONS

The *Schomberg,* described as "the noblest ship that ever
floated upon the water", was the pride of British
shipbuilding; its captain, the daredevil "Bully" Forbes,
dreamed of reaching Melbourne in sixty days. But her loss
off Curdie's River, on the southern tip of Australia, on her
maiden voyage in 1855 spelt not only her end but his, and
set in motion a chain of enquiries, recriminations and
rumours.

But no Australian wreck is as well remembered as that of
the *Loch Ard;* her loss is one of the great tragic and
romantic stories. There were only two survivors — a girl of
eighteen, Eva Carmichael, and Tom Pearce, about the same
age, an apprentice, who saved her life. Their poignant story
ultimately precipitated the end of the era of
passenger-carrying sailing ships and the turn to the new
safety of steam.

Don Charlwood, himself a descendant of a survivor from
the wreck of the *Schomberg,* brings together the mysterious
tale of the *Schomberg's* loss and the story of the *Loch Ard,*
from his earlier book *The Wreck of the Loch Ard,* in a
compelling and highly readable record of the colonial
clipper era and its effects on the history of the southern tip
of Australia.

Also by Don Charlwood

No Moon Tonight
All the Green Year
An Afternoon of Time
Take-off to Touchdown
The Wreck of the Loch Ard (later incorporated in Wrecks and
Reputations)
Settlers under Sail
Flight and Time
The Long Farewell
Marching as to War
Journeys into Night

WRECKS & REPUTATIONS

The Loss of the Schomberg and Loch Ard

Don Charlwood

Burgewood Books
4 Diane Court
Warrandyte
Victoria 3113
Australia

First published by Angus & Robertson Publishers, Australia, 1977
Reprinted 1978
Second Edition 1988
New Edition by Burgewood Books 1996
Reprinted by Burgewood Books 2000

© Don Charlwood 1977

Printed by SRM Production Services Sdn. Bhd.

National Library of Australia
Cataloguing in Publication data

Charlwood, Donald Ernest C.
Wrecks and Reputations.

Index.
ISBN 0 646 28006 6
1. Shipwrecks–Victoria.
I. Title.
919.457

CONTENTS

ILLUSTRATIONS

ACKNOWLEDGEMENTS

The western entrance to Bass Strait, between Cape Otway and Cape Wickham, was a final obstacle for sailing ship masters on the long journey from Europe to the eastern states of Australia, a journey often carried out without an earlier sighting of land. For forty-three years, from the wreck of the *Neva* in 1835, it was an obstacle that brought great loss in lives and ships. By far the greater losses were on the King Island side. On the Victorian side only two passenger ships were lost: the *Schomberg* and the *Loch Ard*; the *Loch Ard*, in fact, was the last sailing ship to lose passengers at the entrance.

It is with these two ships that this book is concerned. To my earlier *Wreck of the Loch Ard* I have linked the story of the *Schomberg* and of her flamboyant master, James Nicol Forbes. I have taken the opportunity to add some newly located material to the *Loch Ard* story and to make some corrections to the earlier book.

This volume is in three sections: "The Western Entrance", " 'Bully' Forbes of the Black Ball Line", and "The Wreck of the *Loch Ard*: End of a Ship, End of an Era". An epilogue and appendixes follow.

For material incorporated in "The Western Entrance" I wish to acknowledge the following sources: Victorian Government year books of the 1850s; letters from C. J. La Trobe to the Colonial Secretary relating to the proposed lighthouse at Cape Otway; Mitchell Library files on lighthouses 47/4793 and 48/6612; papers of the Legislative Council of New South Wales (Mitchell Library 45/38); State Library of Tasmania documents CSO 24/236/9159; Victorian Government Gazette for 29.7.1846; correspondence books of Cape Otway Lighthouse (Department of Transport); two articles by George R. Leggett—"History of Bass Strait" (*Victorian Historical Magazine*, vol. 25, 1953); article by Alexander Sutherland, "Wreck of the Cataraqui"; Leslie Norman's *Sea Wolves and Bandits*; Geoffrey Blainey's *Tyranny of Distance*; Michael Cannon's *Who's Master? Who's Man?*

In " 'Bully' Forbes of the Black Ball Line": The Geelong Historical Society's "*Lightning*" *Diary of John Fenwick* (1854); Basil Lubbock's *Colonial Clippers*; article by Cecil Johnson, "Exploits of the Notorious 'Bully' Forbes (Melbourne *Argus*, undated clipping); the following London Public Record Office documents relating to ships and seamen—Transcripts and Transactions Series II (BT108), Certificates of Competency Book, Register of Seamen Black Book. The following papers from the Liverpool City Libraries: address by Captain E. A. Woods to the Liverpool Nautical Research Society, 1943; article by Dr George Chandler, "Men Who Made Liverpool Great" (*Liverpool Echo and Evening Express*, 31/5/1961); *Last Hours on the Mersey, or Forget-Me-Not* (1855); Warren Armstrong's *Tales of Tall Ships*; Joseph Foley's *Three Liverpool Worthies*; contemporary Liverpool newspaper reports of Forbes's voyages. This London and Liverpool material concerning Forbes I have lodged with the La Trobe Library, Melbourne. Lodged also with that library are reports on Forbes's last wreck obtained from the South African Library, Cape Town. Similarly, numerous Melbourne newspaper reports concerning Forbes's voyages and his court hearings, all provided by the La Trobe Library, have been lodged with the Liverpool City Libraries. I am indebted also to Mr W. Forbes Mann of Liverpool, great-grandson of Captain Forbes and to Mr Baden Norris of Christchurch for information concerning the section of the *Schomberg* that drifted to New Zealand.

In "The Wreck of the *Loch Ard*" section: Basil Lubbock's *Colonial Clippers*; Margaret MacKenzie's *Shipwrecks*; Richard Bennett's compilation, *Narrative of the Wreck of the*

Ship Loch Ard (1890); "The Legendary Loch Liners" (*Port of Melbourne Quarterly*, 1953); "Reminiscences of Hugh Hamilton Gibson: a Pioneer" (*Victorian Historical Magazine*, June 1957); the Gibson family papers, by favour of Mr Hugh Sloane and the Heytesbury District Historical Society; article by George Johnston, "Hoodoo Ship *Loch Ard*" (*Sea Breezes*, March 1932); *Port Campbell and its Attractions* (a local publication containing William Till's story); script of radio talk on the *Loch Ard* given in the mid-1930s by Horace Bedggood; Salvage Statement of Ship *Loch Ard* by favour of Mr S. C. Grant, Benalla; Marine Board enquiries 1857-76; contemporary newspaper reports from Melbourne, Sydney, Warrnambool, and Colac provided by the La Trobe Library.

Several bodies proved most generous with their assistance in all sections of the book: the National Maritime Museum, Greenwich; the Royal Historical Society of Victoria; the Public Records Office, Melbourne; Furness Withy and Company Limited (successors to the Loch Line); the City of Warrnambool Library; the Australian Public Service Archives, Melbourne; Shaw, Savill and Albion Ltd.

Many people who have had long interest in sailing ships have been helpful and patient in providing technical information. Particularly I wish to mention the late Mr John Shelden, of the Ship Lovers' Society, Melbourne; also Mr Bedford Osborne of Gundaroo, New South Wales, for his reconstruction of the last manoeuvres of the *Loch Ard*; Captain G. A. Molyneux and Mr Hartley Watson, of Melbourne; Miss S. A. E. Strom, editor of the Ship Lovers' *Dog Watch*; Miss Jean MacKenzie; Miss Innes Cameron; Mr John Gould and Mr John K. Loney.

Information came from several people who live on the west coast of Victoria and from others who are interested in its history: Mr Stan McPhee and his co-worker on wrecks, Mr Don Baird; Mr Athol Bowker; Mr and Mrs Selwyn Duruz; Mr Donald Walker; the late Mrs Thornton Grimwade; Mrs L. F. Keiller; Mr T. Wicking. Others had family links with those involved in the aftermath of the wreck of the *Loch Ard*; or with victims: Mr John George Gibb and Mrs Grace English, of Queensland, relatives of Captain George Gibb;

Mesdames Elsie Clarendon and Anne Fuller, daughters of Jane Osborne, who helped care for Eva Carmichael; Miss Kathleen Green, a relative of Eva Carmichael; Mr. Colin McArthur, grandson of Peter McArthur, of Glenample. Information on an earlier era came from the Buckby family of Tasmania concerning thier great-grandfather, David Howie, Special Constable of the Bass Strait Islands.

Charts were drawn by Mr. Richard Gosden; the navigational detail check by Mr. John Walsh. To all of these people and organizations, my sincere thanks.

Don Charlwood

ACKNOWLEDGMENTS TO 1996 EDITION

Mr. Alan Horth of Canberra has traced the ship's papers of the *Loch Ard* to the University of Newfoundland and has thus been able to provide a crew and passenger list as close to correct as is now possible. He also obtained from Dr. William Gibb, a great-nephew of Captain Gibb, a copy of Captain Gibb's marriage certificate. This shows that his bride's maiden name was McMeekan, not Carmichael as reported in the Australian press. These corrections have been made to this edition. My thanks to Mr. Horth and also to Liz Wilks for revision to the chart of the Western Entrance to Bass Strait.

D.C.

AUTHOR'S NOTE

When the *Schomberg* ran aground off Curdie's River on the night of Boxing Day 1855, the passengers were in no great peril, even though the magnificent ship itself was doomed. But no luggage could be taken off by them. One family of seven were bidden by their mother to put on all the extra clothes they could wear. The mother was Mary Lewis, bringing her children from London to join their father in Melbourne. The eldest, Emily Lewis, then seventeen, recalled on her ninetieth birthday, "We were not allowed to take any of our belongings —so I put on two dresses. It was before the days of crinolines, but we wore skirts six yards round, with three or more stiff petticoats to hold them out". Sixty years after the wreck I was added to the already very large number of her grandchildren. In addition to their numerous layers of clothes, the family only retrieved a punch bowl and a fruit bowl; both have remained with descendants in Melbourne.

When my grandmother was approaching her end at the age of ninety-six, she spoke still of watching the bows of the *Schomberg* splintering on the reef that now bears its name. Her stories drew me to the area in 1934, first to Cape Otway itself. At that time the only way to the lighthouse was still by La Trobe's "tolerable road" which I picked up three miles out of Apollo Bay. I wrote later:

It dropped into the valley of the Elliott River, descending into forest. In the mud were long skid marks where the lighthouse keepers coming from Apollo Bay had slid beside their horses to the bottom, since it was too steep to ride. I laboured up walls of mud and around butts of trees, up out of the Elliott then down into the Geary. Where the valleys ended the forest also ended and the country became a wilderness of scrub with sand underfoot. Here and there wallabies crossed the track, but there was scarcely a movement from anything else and scarcely a sign that anyone ever came there. Twelve miles out I topped a high ridge and saw grassland rolling to the south and the lighthouse itself still five or six miles off on the brink of the sea, caught between the sea and the grassy dunes and inland scrub. The sight of it all at once was arresting and in some way comforting—its formal lines and its whiteness perhaps, after the formless grey-green of forest and scrub. And it was in some way moving to reflect that in the first days men had struggled there to bring safety; to remember, too, that immigrants who had boarded ships in the Thames and Mersey had there first seen their new country, their eyes turning to this shaft as the only sign of settlement. From the next hill I could see keepers' cottages clustered at the base of the shaft, deserted-looking and braced against the wind.

On that first visit to the lighthouse I was shown a chart on which the wrecks at the western entrance had been plotted. I began to ask then why there were so many. It was a question that led me eventually to gather the material for this book. With awareness of its inadequacies, I dedicate it now to the memory of Mary Lewis and the seven children who emigrated with her on the *Schomberg*.

DON CHARLWOOD

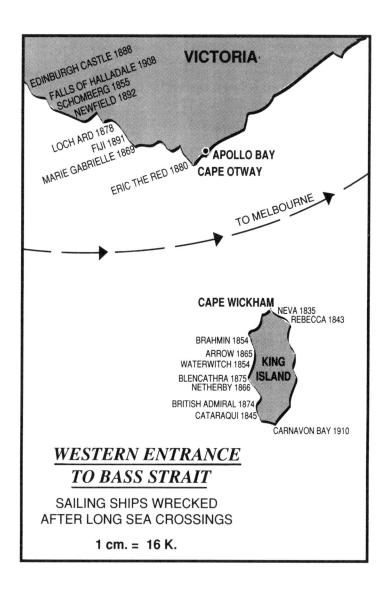

EDINBURGH CASTLE 1888
FALLS OF HALLADALE 1908
SCHOMBERG 1855
NEWFIELD 1892

VICTORIA·

LOCH ARD 1878
FIJI 1891
MARIE GABRIELLE 1869
ERIC THE RED 1880

● APOLLO BAY
CAPE OTWAY

TO MELBOURNE

CAPE WICKHAM
NEVA 1835
REBECCA 1843

BRAHMIN 1854
ARROW 1865
WATERWITCH 1854
BLENCATHRA 1875
NETHERBY 1866
BRITISH ADMIRAL 1874
CATARAQUI 1845

KING ISLAND

CARNAVON BAY 1910

WESTERN ENTRANCE
TO BASS STRAIT

SAILING SHIPS WRECKED
AFTER LONG SEA CROSSINGS

1 cm. = 16 K.

THE WESTERN ENTRANCE

1
THE TOLL

In the seas around Cape Otway and Cape Wickham lie the remains of over fifty ships—sealers, convict transports, immigrant clippers, coastal traders. Charts have been drawn showing their names clustered at the western entrance of Bass Strait, some piled on cliffs and reefs around Cape Otway, others on the west coast of King Island. The first large passenger ship lost on the Otway side was the *Schomberg*, commanded on her 1855 maiden voyage by James Nicol Forbes, until then probably the greatest of clipper captains. In the *Marco Polo* he had set a record between Liverpool and Melbourne of sixty-eight days and in the *Lightning* a return record around Cape Horn of sixty-three days—times and circumstances even more impressive than those attending the London–Sydney–London race of 1975. But the maiden voyage of the *Schomberg* spelled her end and his when, unaccountably, he lost her off Curdie's River.

The last passenger ship lost at the Bass Strait entrance was the *Loch Ard* in 1878. Her loss may be said to have closed the era of passenger-carrying sailing ships on the Australian run. The trade had been dwindling for years in the face of competition from steam. Although a trickle of passengers continued to travel by sail after the wreck of the *Loch Ard*, sail's real day was done. Here in one ship and even in one ill-fated family, the hazards faced by immigrants of the vanishing era are revealed as by a lightning flash. Australians were shocked that such a calamity could still occur so close to home.

In the life of Eva Carmichael, the only passenger to survive the wreck of the *Loch Ard*, one may see epitomized the changing attitude of emigrants to sail. When she had recovered sufficiently from her ordeal to be able to return to Britain, she returned by steam. The thought of travelling again by sailing ship was abhorrent to her. Her experience, and the experiences of other victims of shipwreck, undoubtedly did much to turn intending emigrants to steam. The day when passengers were willing to entrust their lives to redoubtable masters of clipper ships was done. Virtually ended, too, was a period of nearly eighty years during which arriving passengers had good reason to fear the Cape Otway landfall.

Of the many sailing ships that failed to negotiate the entrance between Cape Otway and King Island, eighteen were nearing the end of long ocean voyages. Their names now read like an honour roll of the fallen in the struggle between sail and this hostile stretch of sea: *Neva*, 1835; *Rebecca*, 1843; *Cataraqui*, 1845; *Brahmin*, 1854; *Waterwitch*, 1854; *Schomberg*, 1855; *Arrow*, 1865; *Netherby*, 1866; *Marie Gabrielle*, 1869; *British Admiral*, 1874; *Blencathra*, 1875; *Loch Ard*, 1878; *Eric the Red*, 1880; *Edinburgh Castle*, 1888; *Fiji*, 1891; *Newfield*, 1892; *Falls of Halladale*, 1908; *Carnarvon Bay*, 1910. The first of the eighteen was a convict transport; the last six were cargo vessels.

On the *Schomberg* no lives were lost; on the *Loch Ard*, fifty-two. Tragic though the case of the *Loch Ard* was, loss of life on the *Neva* was four times as bad, on the *Cataraqui* nearly six times; the *Fiji* involved suffering much more prolonged and a degree of heroism on the part of two midshipmen that was not matched even in the *Loch Ard* disaster.

Why were they lost, all these ships? If one seeks to answer this question, much is learnt of the background to many a last voyage. Underlying causes ranged from difficulties of navigation to demands by shipping companies for speed and more speed; from peril of storms to a final difficult landfall. In Forbes's day a master could often truly declare, "I sailed out of Liverpool, first landfall, Otway!" At Otway itself there was enormous difficulty in establishing a lighthouse. Lives would have been saved could it have been established earlier.

2
A SHORT CUT

The era that closed in Bass Strait with the wreck of the *Loch Ard* had begun in 1800. Bass and Flinders had discovered the strait in 1798. Their discovery caused immediate interest in Britain since it promised to cut seven hundred miles off the journey to Sydney and give a final passage less boisterous than the rounding of Van Diemen's Land.

In 1800 Lieutenant James Grant, on his way from England to Sydney in the sixty-ton *Lady Nelson*, was intercepted at Cape Town by a ship homeward bound from Australia. It carried instructions for him: he was to endeavour to pass through Bass Strait from the west. This he did in December of that year, the first master known to have passed between Cape Otway and Cape Wickham. Cape Otway he named, but Cape Wickham he did not sight, nor did he see any other part of King Island. The island was named in the next month by Captain Black, east-bound in the *Harbinger*, the second ship to negotiate the strait from the west.

It is possible that Grant was preceded by sealers, for they were attracted like vultures by Bass and Flinders' report of large colonies of seals and sea elephants on the islands and rocks of the strait. By 1802 it was estimated that over two hundred sealers had settled themselves on the outlying islands. The spoils were tempting: one ship's crew alone killed 4300 seals and six hundred sea elephants in a month.

As time passed, American sealers joined in the slaughter. Although their activity was resented in Sydney, little could be done to counter it. But it is noticeable that the Government tended to turn a blind eye on the escape of convicts from the newly established penal settlements in Van Diemen's Land. If they survived in their cockleshell boats, these escapees often turned to sealing on the islands, thus augmenting the numerous adventurers and runaway sailors already there. A local breed of "Straitsmen" grew up, a fearfully hardened race who raided the mainland coast to abduct native "wives". They disposed of their spoils to sealing ships doing the round of the islands; the Americans they resented bitterly.

Since the Straitsmen had become exceedingly skilful handlers of small boats in difficult seas and were men who put little value on human life, they seem to have bested the intruders in a series of bloody encounters. Finally the Americans left them undisputed rulers of the straits and moved their own operations to the relative safety of Western Australia.

After Grant's passage past Otway, thirty-four years were to elapse before the Hentys settled at Portland Bay; thirty-five before Melbourne was founded. The only Europeans to visit the mainland coast were whalers and Straitsmen sealers. There was consequently no prospect at all of building a lighthouse at Cape Otway, though it was recognized that one was sorely needed to mark the entrance to the newly charted strait.

In those years before Melbourne was founded, and before serious consideration could be given to erecting a landfall lighthouse, the straits saw a considerable amount of shipping. Many of these early ships were convict transports. Some idea of living conditions aboard them may be gauged by averaging the tonnage of eleven transports that passed through the strait during the year 1831 and comparing this with the average number of souls each ship carried: average tonnage 515; average souls carried 209.

It is remarkable that few of these ships were lost. Probably this was because their masters, unlike masters of later years, were not hard pressed to make fast passages and therefore tended to hug the mainland coast and not proceed until they were sure of their position.

There was one fearful exception to this relatively good record: in 1835, a month before the arrival of Batman in

Port Phillip, the transport *Neva*, bringing a wretched cargo of convict women and their children from Cork, was totally lost on King Island. Only twenty-two of her complement of 241 reached shore; seven of these died of starvation.

In 1841 the Governor of Van Diemen's Land, Sir John Franklin, urged the Government of New South Wales to consider the erection of lighthouses in Bass Strait. The ensuing Select Committee recommended King Island in preference to Cape Otway as the place for a guiding light to the western entrance, but the scheme was shelved because of the depressed state of the economy at the time. King Island had to wait twenty years for its Wickham light.

The straits were not only perilous navigationally; there was always the prospect, if a ship was wrecked, that it would be swiftly pillaged by Straitsmen wreckers. Wreckers' caches have been uncovered by shifts of sand on King Island even in recent years.

The only effective steps taken to safeguard life and property at the western end of Bass Strait were initiated by David Howie, a Scottish-born farmer, trader, and sealer who settled on Robbins Island, off the north-west tip of Van Diemen's Land, in 1840. As a voluntary task he visited the major islands each quarter, keeping watch for victims of shipwreck. Bishop Nixon, who came to Van Diemen's Land in 1854, spoke of Howie as "an enterprising and skilful mariner, also a singularly intelligent man".

Howie first gained prominence in connection with the wreck of the *Cataraqui*, which occurred six years after the appointment to Port Phillip District of Superintendent La Trobe. La Trobe was already acutely aware of the need for a lighthouse at Cape Otway, but the Great Southern Forest and the Barrier Range—later the Otway Forest and the Otway Ranges—had not been penetrated by the settlers.

The wreck of the *Cataraqui* was the type of disaster of which La Trobe must have lived in dread. An emigrant ship, bound from Liverpool to Melbourne, she had run for several days before a storm. She carried 370 passengers and a crew of thirty-eight. On the evening of 3rd August 1845, knowing that he must be nearing the entrance to Bass Strait, the captain shortened sail, apparently hoping to establish his position at dawn.

It has been recorded that antagonism existed between the captain and the surgeon all through the voyage. The surgeon was eager for the journey to end as quickly as possible, since the outbreak of an epidemic would have meant loss of bounty money payable to him for delivering the immigrants in good health. When sail was shortened on the approach to Bass Strait, the surgeon reputedly ridiculed the captain's caution. Nettled, the captain put on sail and the *Cataraqui* drove on during the night. Before dawn she struck the south-western end of King Island. Of a total of 408 souls on board, only nine reached shore alive.

On Robbins Island a rosewood couch was washed ashore. This was found by David Howie, who, from his knowledge of the straits, deduced that a wreck had occurred on King Island. It was eleven days after the disaster when he at last found the wretched survivors—the chief officer, seven of the crew, and one passenger—on a beach strewn with bodies and wreckage for two miles. Howie was chiefly responsible for the burial of over two hundred bodies in four large graves.

It was probably this action that led to government recognition of Howie's extraordinary work. In 1847 he was dubbed Special Constable of the Bass Strait Islands and given the assistance of "two Petty Constables from Launceston".

In 1853, because of the numerous shipwrecks in the straits, the residents of the Circular Head district of Van Diemen's Land sent a petition to the Lieutenant-Governor asking that Howie be given official authority over the islands of the straits and be provided with every facility needed for his work. The petition was refused.

Howie's own life ended six years later. In May 1859 three escaped convicts reached his home on Robbins Island. He had time to conceal his wife and three daughters under a table draped with a large cloth. Hidden there, they heard the convicts demand at pistol point that Howie ferry them to the mainland—a formidable journey even for him. The four set out and were never seen again.

3
ESTABLISHING THE LIGHT

In Melbourne the many detractors of La Trobe did not hesitate to blame him most unfairly for loss of the *Cataraqui*. When news of the disaster reached England, the Admiralty sounded warnings against use of Bass Strait:

Each year has been marked by more or less loss of life, and the last mail from Sydney adds to the catalogue an account of the wreck of the *Cataraqui*. . . . My lords will consider it their duty to prevent transports with troops or convicts to attempt navigating the said straits till light-houses have been built and they would recommend that emigrant ships also be prohibited from navigating them for the same period.

Already further inquiry in Sydney had changed the 1841 committee's preference for King Island, and Cape Otway was recommended as the place for a landfall light. This was probably for two reasons: mariners preferred to cling to the bold Otway coast, for King Island lies dangerously low in the sea; also Cape Wickham, the island's northernmost tip, is buttressed by outlying reefs.

Following the *Cataraqui* disaster, the New South Wales Government urged La Trobe to find a route to Cape Otway. Erection of a lighthouse there was now imperative. La Trobe scarcely needed the urging. Twice in 1845 he led parties into the Great Southern Forest, and on both occasions returned with his horses exhausted. He had pushed far into the forest but under the canopy of mountain ash he had found ranges of such steepness that often the horses could not be ridden. Dense undergrowth hampered progress and reduced visibility to a few yards.

Early in 1846, on a third attempt, La Trobe reached the cape on foot by skirting the forest to the west. On this journey he went right out onto the cape: " . . . we have really found Cape Otway. Receding line of coast on both sides—east to Cape Patton and west to Moonlight Head". Although he declared that "the brink of the precipitous face of the Southern point of the promontory furnishes, as it appears to me, an admirable site for the projected lighthouse", he realized that the route by which he had reached it was useless as a practicable entry to the site:

The coastline from the westward, by which I reached the Cape on foot, however open as far as Moonlight Head, is totally impracticable for horses or oxen beyond that headland. The precipitous and rugged character of the rocky spurs of the mountains abutting upon the straits, and the depth of the wooded ravines, which must be passed in attempting to cross them, form serious impediments to approach in any manner. I fear from all I ascertain that approach along the Eastern coast will be found to be equally impracticable. From the westward the Cape is equally unapproachable by sea. In sixty miles of coast in that direction there is certainly no more than one boat harbour and that so far from the Cape as to be useless.

This was Port Campbell, thirty-two miles off by sea, a diminutive harbour providing inadequate shelter and separated from Cape Otway by the most dangerous part of the coast. It had been named in the earliest years of the century after Captain Campbell, a man dubbed "the last of the buccaneers", who is reputed to have entered it in pursuit of a whale.

There was no alternative for La Trobe but to attempt the forest route a third time. On this occasion he nominated "Mr Allan of the Hopkins" as leader of the party. Again the project was thwarted. On 4th June 1846 La Trobe informed the Colonial Secretary that "the party appointed . . . to seek a line of road accessible to horses or oxen from the Colac District, have finally returned to the Border Police Station [between Colac and the Stony Rises], after being out from first to last thirty-two days, without having succeeded."

Nevertheless the party under Allan had marked a "tolerable

road" across the Barrier Range and had come within five or six miles of the cape. "At that point Allan found further progress at this season impossible from the impracticable character of the ravines."

La Trobe's dispatch contained one better piece of news: Mr George Smythe had surveyed the coast from the sea and had made a detailed survey of Cape Otway itself. A landing place had been determined.

Although the land party had failed, much credit must go to Allan for the final establishment of a road to Cape Otway. Late in the winter of 1846 another settler, William Roadknight of Yan Yan Gurt, a property south-west of Geelong, pushed the road through to the cape and continued farther. He took up land in the valley of the Aire River; this holding he named Glen Aire.

Although La Trobe had used the term "tolerable road", it was scarcely that. For half the fifty miles from Colac it followed razorbacks above the Barwon River, then in ten miles dropped two thousand feet from Mount Sabine to the mouth of Skene's Creek in Apollo Bay. It followed the shore of the bay, then paralleled the coast about two miles inland for most of the remaining fifteen miles to the cape.

The "tolerable road" was in fact no more than a tenuous link with civilization, subject to fire and flood, its gradients so steep that in places bullocks had to be given winching assistance by means of cables anchored to butts of trees. Its mud was exhausting to both oxen and drivers, and the forest imprisoned its few travellers in a world of green gloom.

But with the "road" put through, La Trobe was ready to build the lighthouse. The Government suggested that he should procure convict labour from Van Diemen's Land, but this the penal authorities refused. In October 1846 the tender of Alexander McGillvray was accepted and work was begun. Eight months later La Trobe ordered an inspection, directing that "two of the native police . . . accompany Mr Burns, of the Clerk of Works' office, as far as the track through the southern forest may be practicable at this season for horses, onto the Cape itself if circumstances permit". Burns struggled through, but found little sign of progress. La Trobe foreclosed on the contract and the Government took over construction itself.

In November 1847 two men were sent overland with bullock drays. At about the same time a working party of forty-three tradesmen left Geelong in the schooner *Teazer*. The Melbourne *Argus* reported the venture: "The master of the vessel, Captain Rogers, while endeavouring to find a landing place was left on shore with his boat's crew, a gale having sprung up which prevented his rejoining the vessel." Next day, "the master and his crew put off their boat although the weather was far from favourable. Unfortunately, in passing through the surf the boat was upset and the master was drowned; the other men were able to reach the shore."

But the workmen were landed and construction of the lighthouse began. It was a relatively short shaft—fifty-two feet—since the cliffs on which it was built were over 250 feet high. It was constructed of sandstone quarried at the Parker River, three miles to the east, and hauled to the site by bullock teams.

Nine months later the lantern—"manufactured by Mr Wilkins of London who made the lantern in use in Eddystone lighthouse"— was delivered by one of Benjamin Boyd's ships and landed through the surf. It was erected three hundred feet above the sea and on 29th August 1848 was lighted—the second lighthouse on the mainland coast. In it were twenty-one parabolic reflectors, each with its own wick lamp burning sperm oil, the whole rotated by clockwork, giving a single flash lasting three seconds in every fifty-three. "Captain Gregurtha of the *Hero* says it is of great strength and brilliance and will be seen at considerable distance." The sight of this new symmetrical white shaft must have comforted many a forlorn immigrant, for here was sign that some of his own kind had blazed a way before him.

The working party packed and sailed away, glad to escape the forest and isolation and incessant roar of sea. They left behind Captain Lawrence, R.N., with two keepers.

Within four months Lawrence had been reported by one of his subordinates for "effecting repairs for which he was not qualified". He was summarily dismissed. His replacement was Henry Bayles Ford, a merchant captain aged thirty, who was appointed at a salary of £120 a year. "My family consists of my wife and two small children, one seven years old, the other two years." Together they were to remain in that isolated place between forest and sea for thirty years. Four more Ford children were to know the lighthouse cottage as their first home.

Ford was a dauntless individual, self-reliant, firm in his dealing with others, and dedicated to his task of bringing a measure of safety to the western entrance. Unfortunately his daily journals prior to 1860 and after 1877 have been lost, but his correspondence books, in which he copied inward and outward letters and official minutes to his staff, have survived. As one might expect of a man holding such a position in such an age, his letters hardly murmur against isolation or hard living, or any other difficulties of such a life, unless these difficulties bear directly upon the service he was there to provide.

Ford went out ahead of his wife. Milk and butter he lacked entirely; meat he was told to procure from "Mr Roadknight's station until that gentleman delivers you the four head of fat cattle due by him to the Government or until the Government are in a position to forward cattle."

Instructions of this nature were sent to Ford from Melbourne by Aboriginal trooper; not infrequently they arrived weeks late. One dated 8th June, for instance, stated, "I enclose herewith my instruction No. 103 of 29th April last which a native trooper attempted to convey to you, but in consequence of the swollen state of the river, was unable to reach Otway." As a result of such delays Ford was unable to have many of his difficulties remedied in his settling-in period. At times he and his wife and the other keepers' families were out of meat, for Roadknight's main interest was in Yan Yan Gurt, and for as long as eighteen months at a time Glen Aire would be unoccupied.

From the beginning of Ford's Otway service, the attitude he was to adopt to his two assistants was stated explicitly: "When giving orders or instructions to the keepers you will at all times address them by their surnames and maintain the respect due to your situation by having them use the word Sir when replying to or addressing you."

Ford's own superiors in Melbourne were often censorious and untrusting. Why had he retained cooking utensils left behind by the party who had built the lighthouse? The cost of these would be deducted from his pay, "the Government not providing furniture or utensils". Why was his remaining oil short by ten gallons?—this out of hundreds of gallons landed through surf in barrels, hauled up from the Parker River and poured into a lamp that leaked. Why had he allowed the light to function imperfectly?

Each charge he rebutted patiently. In answering the last he added, "I can observe the light while lying in my bed and more especially this last two months as I have been continually kept from sleep being troubled with severe toothache."

Mrs Ford was Irish, having come originally from Wexford as governess to the children of Superintendent La Trobe. She could have had little idea of life in such a place as Otway. She had been there four years and had borne more children before Ford wrote: "As it is very difficult to obtain a supply of milk and butter at the Cape and . . . the same being a severe hardship on my family, you will be conferring a great benefit on the establishment by granting permission to run a few head of cows at the Cape." The cows were granted them.

For the most part the surviving lighthouse journals are a record of weather and the wearying round of polishing glass, filling lamps, trimming wicks, painting the lighthouse and its cottages, obtaining firewood, settling arguments; but over the years there are occasional dramatic happenings. On the evening of 5th December 1860 "I heard by the telegraph from Apollo Bay that the body of the line repairer F. Lee was found half way between here on the line. He was black in the face. Supposed to have been dead 36 or 48 hours and either died by snake bite or a fit." Years later, on 28th November 1869, "late in the afternoon my young son came running home shouting that he had seen four men coming from [the west]. The other son came home later and informed me that there was a wreck and that these four men had left 7 others behind and that they had not any food for four days." This was the wreck of the *Marie Gabrielle*, which had occurred on 24th November, a day of "strong gales, southerly with rain". She was a French ship bound for Melbourne from Foochow. On 7th December Ford noted, "The shipwrecked crew left this morning for Apollo Bay with three days provisions accompanied by Mr Lawry and four horses."

One of the two Ford boys who came upon the shipwrecked Frenchmen was George, then aged twelve. Nine years later he was to play a prominent part in the aftermath of the *Loch Ard* disaster.

4
GOLD MANIA

In 1851, the year gold was discovered in Ballarat, 712 ships arrived in Victoria from overseas and gold to the value of £580,548 was mined. In the next year 1657 ships arrived and the value of gold mined rose to £10,953,936. A decade of gold had begun. The administration of the colony was overwhelmed. Edward Grimes, Immigration Agent in Melbourne, struggling to keep his head above the flood, addressed an urgent memorandum to La Trobe:

So far from this torrent of Immigration being likely to decrease, each succeeding month shews increase in the number and tonnage of vessels arriving in the harbour. Intelligence reaches the Colony by every fresh arrival of scores upon scores of ships laid on for this Colony, not only from England, but from almost every portion of the habitable world— a large part of them being devoted solely to the conveyance of passengers; and it is much to be regretted that a large proportion of the population so introduced is of a class utterly unfitted for the hard labor of gold digging, and who have entirely overrated the capabilities of the Colony for affording remunerative employment to persons of the educated classes, while the hardships which the crowded state of the city entails upon many of them, will, I fear, be productive of much misery.

Melbourne could not "furnish even temporary shelter to the myriads now landing daily on our shores".

Grimes's concern could do nothing in the short term to ease the problem, but considering the colonial administrators across the years, one can admire most of them for their efforts to improve the lot of the immigrants. From the Home government they sought more careful selection of assisted emigrants, safer ships, better supervision on the way out. Some of their counterparts in Britain showed evidence of concern, but it was an era in which private enterprise was largely free of government intervention. More money was to be made by the owners of unseaworthy ships than any miner could make from gold. Samuel Plimsoll, "the sailor's friend", had not yet campaigned effectively against sending to sea deliberately overloaded, heavily insured ships. If such ships disappeared with all hands, their loss was easy money in rapacious owners' pockets.

In the colony of Victoria one man, years ahead of his time, was protesting against the state of affairs. James Ballingall, who had run ships himself and was a ship surveyor, had been dismayed by what he had witnessed on his own passage out. He was instrumental in setting up in Melbourne the Anti-Shipwreck Society. But the society's pleas for safer ships and protective legislation, although backed in Australia, fell on deaf ears in England. Shipowners were left free for several years to continue much as they pleased. Not only were ships overloaded, often they were not in a fit state to cover a quarter of the journey they were embarking upon. Women were unsafe, not only among predatory male passengers, but more so among the very officers it was assumed would protect them. There was little semblance of the hygiene at sea fostered as long ago as 1769 by Cook.

When eventually an enquiry was held in England into travelling conditions, an appalling picture emerged:

It was scarcely possible to induce the passengers to sweep the decks after their meals or to be decent in respect to the common wants of nature. In many cases, in bad weather, they would not go on deck, their health suffered so much that their strength was gone, and they had not the power to help themselves. Hence the between decks were like a loathsome dungeon. When hatchways were opened, under which people were stowed, the steam rose and the stench was like that from a pen of pigs. The few beds they had were in a dreadful state, for the straw, once wet with sea water soon rotted, besides which they used the between decks for all sorts of filthy purposes.

In such conditions, and given the standard of medicine of

the day, loss of life aboard these "coffin ships", as crews termed them, was high indeed. And many of the medical superintendents appear to have been more concerned with the bounty they would receive on arrival than with the health of their passengers. The surgeon-superintendent of the *Allison*, for example, on his arrival in Hobson's Bay in December 1852, reported no disease on board when, in fact, he had an outbreak of malignant typhus. There had been fourteen deaths from it during the voyage and there were to be nine more while the ship was in quarantine.

The assumption was made, even by the humane La Trobe, that it was not possible to convey working class people with any semblance of cleanliness from Britain to Australia. No amount of effort, La Trobe believed, could "overcome that repugnance to cleanliness which distinguishes certain classes of the labouring population of Europe". And once disease had taken hold of a ship, "no efforts of the officers in charge would be effective in stemming its progress".

The social structure of Britain in these years has been the subject of innumerable studies. The emigrants' voyage to Australia was simply an extension of it. The gentry, or those sufficiently well-to-do to lay claim to it, travelled saloon; the lower orders, steerage, often little better regarded than the convicts who had preceded them and whose refurbished transports they often used. If the ship was wrecked, the distinctions were likely to be maintained: lifeboats for saloon passengers were reasonably assured; for steerage they might not even exist.

In retrospect it seems extraordinary that these divisions were so generally accepted on both sides as a "natural order", ordained by the Creator. The ship's master and his officers, men "drest in a little brief authority", were the seagoing representatives of the Establishment's order. Many tyrannized the passengers least able to fend for themselves, people from impoverished homes who often were unable to read or write and were utter strangers to the sea.

But master and officers were themselves men under orders. Their employers expected them to reach the colony with all speed possible, slowing for nothing, neither burial of the dead nor pleas of the alarmed living. A quick passage advertised their company to the thousands waiting for the next voyage, and the next and the next. Gold mined in Victoria in 1853 exceeded £12 million. Hunger for it had driven all sense from people's minds.

At Cape Otway the unfortunate Ford called it "the gold mania" as his assistants deserted him for the diggings. "Duties of a threefold and heavily responsible nature were devolved upon myself for periods of three or four months." Because of the isolated nature of his station, Ford asked that he be sent "no expirees", but during the gold-rush reliable men were difficult to recruit and some who did agree to go out found the life, or even the journey, too much to bear. "R. H. Cant reached Geelong when lost heart and William Harroway is sent in his stead." "Keeper Thomas Rickett proceeds from the lighthouse to Geelong or Melbourne tomorrow," wrote Ford. "His wife [h]as become insane and is very dangerous attempting to destroy herself and infant. I have requested him to remove her to the asylum." Through the forest Rickett must have gone, and over the uninhabited ranges, leading on another horse his deranged wife. It is difficult to conceive of more pitiful travellers. And there was Thomas Lamb, who after long hours of extra duty flew into a rage and called Ford "disgracefull names such as tyrannical bloody wretch" and thrust his fist into Ford's shirt "while having in it a pair of scissors".

But the light, with its twenty-one wicks to be lighted and trimmed each night, was kept burning. Overseas ships, eastbound and west-bound, were passing the cape at the rate of ten a day. At Port Phillip Heads they had the services of a pilot, but as they made landfall at the western entrance of Bass Strait they had nothing but Ford's lighthouse. There, briefly, two men unknown to each other in person would hold responsibility between them for scores of passengers: the master of the passing ship and Ford, immobile at his light. Separated by a few miles of sea, invisible to each other and unable to exchange salutations, the minds of both would be thankful that one more ship had safely entered the strait.

5
A FASTER PASSAGE

In Europe, as thousands strove to reach Victoria before the gold was worked out, competing shipping companies had to find ways of achieving faster passages if they were to continue to attract their share of the spoils. One answer was to design speedier ships. At this time, ships combining the greatest strength and speed were coming from Nova Scotia and Boston, particularly from the Boston yards of Donald McKay, who was himself a Nova Scotian. Scottish craftsmen had settled in the Maritime Provinces of Canada late in the eighteenth century and had begun shipbuilding there for the British trade. Their large softwood clippers, carrying acres of sail, were capable of sustaining high speeds for men who could handle them. With yacht-like bows and raked masts over a hundred and fifty feet high, carrying clouds of canvas, they were probably the most beautiful vessels man ever created. But their vast area of canvas harnessed the wind to such a degree that they needed the most expert handling to avoid disaster. And, like all sailing ships, if the wind was against them they could only progress by tacking. The great fear of masters was being caught unawares close to a lee shore, the wind pressing them toward rocks or shoals. The more confined the area, the less hope there was of manoeuvring out. No ships devised by man were more complex than the clippers. Each sail, each mast and rope and piece of equipment bore an ancient name, many of them now forgotten. These terms were the working language of crews.

The overriding desire of travellers was to get to the goldfields as quickly as possible; discomfort on board ship was something to be suffered—though it often proved worse than anything they had imagined. Generally they were provided with no more than bare cabin space which they were required to furnish for themselves. Often the ship raced with decks awash and three or four men grappling with the wheel. Huddled below deck, the potential miners must often have listened with foreboding to the wash and batter of waves and the shouted orders. They could only put their trust in the godlike master, a man required to bawl his orders against the din of the sea and the wind shrieking in the rigging, so that officers could relay them around the ship. Small wonder that some such men became tyrants.

Speed was increased and discomfort worsened when a new route was devised. It cut a thousand miles off the journey, but for much of its way it lay in the giant waves of the Southern Indian Ocean. This was the composite great circle route.

Advanced cartographers had known for years that the straight routes drawn on the familiar Mercator's chart were by no means the shortest distance between destinations. Because the earth is a sphere, the shortest distance between two points on its surface is the arc of the great circle connecting them. A "great circle" splits the earth into two equal halves. The meridians are thus great circles; so, too, is the equator. But to follow an arc between places not on the equator, or not on the same meridian, involved other problems.

It was evident that the greatest saving in distance on the run to Australia would be made when a ship was heading west to east. But actually to follow a great circle was impossible, for it dipped over part of the Antarctic continent. The best compromise would be to go as far south as icebergs allowed.

Icebergs in the southern oceans present a much greater threat than they do in northern oceans. There is no moderating Gulf Stream Drift such as warms the North Atlantic, no North Pacific Drift, only cold currents from the Antarctic which put a belt of cold around the entire globe: the West Wind Drift which brings icebergs up into the roaring forties and, much more so, into the fifties. But the new route deliberately aimed for the fifties. There the winds and waves pass uninterrupted around the earth; gales of wind, mountainous waves. These were hazards that even well-informed Europeans had difficulty in comprehending. After all, they knew that the whole of Britain lay between latitudes fifty and sixty north; London itself was about as far north as they might reach south. Small wonder that most of them were to travel inadequately clad.

There was a further complication in attempting the composite great circle route: using a magnetic compass it was impossible to follow a curve because of its constant change of direction. The solution in this case was to break the curve into a number of straight chords or rhumb-lines. This all looked good on paper, and mariners had realized years before the gold decade that if they could follow such rhumb-lines the time saving would be considerable. But they had no means of knowing when they should change direction onto each successive one. They could only do this if they knew just how far east or west around the world they had come—in other words, if they knew their longitude. Latitude they had long been able to derive from the angle of the sun above the horizon at noon, but longitude meant determining how far east or west of the Greenwich meridian their ship lay.

It was known that this could be determined if a navigator knew what time of day it was at Greenwich at the moment he observed noon on his ship. Since the earth rotates 360 degrees in twenty-four hours, then each hour of difference in time represents 15 degrees around the earth. The solution was tantalizingly obvious, but there was no chronometer accurate enough to keep reliable Greenwich time throughout a voyage. Charles II had offered a prize for such a chronometer, but it was not until 1735 that one was designed which remained little affected by temperature changes and the motion of a ship. Even then, it was not until the time of Cook that chronometers both reliable and of small size were available.

By the time of Victoria's gold decade John Towson, an English watchmaker, had produced a relatively cheap chronometer. Towson was also examiner of ships' masters at Liverpool and, as such, was insistent upon the use of a composite great circle route.

It is difficult to know to whom credit should be given for introducing this route, Towson or the American Matthew Maury. Both appear to have played an important part. Maury was an outstanding authority on winds and oceans. He had long urged mariners to keep as closely as possible to great circle routes. His directions to masters bound for Australia were that they should reach the equator five hundred miles short of Brazil. From there they should head south—probably hoping to see the traditional landfall islands of South Trinidad and Tristan da Cunha—to "about latitude 45°, reaching 55° South, *if at all*, in about 40° East". This meant that the more resolute masters would pass eight hundred miles south of the Cape of Good Hope. "Thence the best course—if ice etc. will allow—is onward still to the southward of east, not caring to get to the northward again of your greatest southern latitude, before reaching 90° East." This is south of Heard Island and less than eight hundred miles from the Antarctic continent. "The course is then north of east, gradually hauling up more and more to the north as you approach Van Diemen's Land. The highest degree of south latitude which it may be prudent to touch, depending mainly on the season of the year and the winds, the state of the ship, and the well-being of the passengers and crew."

If such hazardous directions were to be followed, there was great danger both from icebergs and imperfectly charted islands. Masters trained to a high standard of navigation were essential. It was in maintenance of such standards and in the provision of cheap chronometers that Towson played an indisputable role. Although it is generally held that he urged use of Maury's routes, it will be seen that he was later to claim a more independent role. At all events, men passing through Towson's hands began making dramatic reductions of passage times to Australia. The first was probably Captain Godfrey who, in 1850, sailed the *Constance* from Plymouth to Adelaide in seventy-six days, about half the usual passage time. The routes followed by these men took them far south of both Cape Town and Perth, farther south than passengers had ever sailed before.

In Melbourne Hugh Childers, chairman of the Immigration Board, began to question the wisdom of the route, "unless the immigrants are previously warned of the weather which they will experience, and proper precautions for their health are taken". There was no doubting that in the piercing cold the sick became sicker. Many an emigrant's body, most of them pitifully small, was committed hastily to those restless wastes. Sorrowful though this was, it was less fearful than the fate of ships that struck one of the numerous icebergs or were trapped among them. The *Guiding Star*, with 546 souls on board, last sighted in the mid-Atlantic, was presumed lost in the ice when she failed to arrive in Melbourne. G. F. Schomberg, Emigration Officer at Liverpool, writing of her eighteen months later, stated that icebergs that year—1855—had been farther north than usual. The *Ralph Waller*, he said, had "been in contact with an iceberg" in latitude 48° south. *Contact* is scarcely an adequate word. She had fifteen feet of water in her hold; the hole torn in her was "partially stopped by lowering a sail overboard"; she had abandoned part of her cargo, then the men had pumped for seventy-nine hours. The *Guiding Star*, he concluded, must have met with a similar, but fatal experience. He was right. Hemmed in the ice, all aboard her had frozen to death.

Such were the risks on the composite great circle route to the clippers that sailed it. But if an emigrant survived ice and illness and drowning, his passage to his supposed El Dorado was likely to be a swift one. Inevitably, there was competition for fast passages between leading masters. They became the popular heroes of the day, and many of them undoubtedly enjoyed presenting a colourful personality to their public. But there can be no denying the responsibility they bore.

Towson, who knew all of those masters and mates sailing from Liverpool, was to rate "Bully" Forbes highest among all those who put his theories of great circle sailing into practice.

"BULLY" FORBES
of the
BLACK BALL LINE

6
FORBES OF
ABERDEEN

Between 1852 and the end of 1855 the name of James Nicol Forbes was lauded in households throughout Britain and Australia. More than any other clipper captain he was drawing the two countries closer in time. Families split by emigration had emotions of gratitude and admiration for him. As he reduced sailing times they felt a little nearer kinsmen at the other end of the earth. And Forbes did it so spectacularly. But in the last month of 1855 his career began its swift decline when he lost the *Schomberg*, "the noblest ship that ever floated upon the water", as he himself described her. He lost her on her maiden voyage a day's sail from Melbourne, on a calm moonlit night. There was no loss of life, but the ship became a total loss off Curdie's River.

Many a time, standing on the dunes not far from the place where the *Schomberg* struck, looking across the few hundred yards of shallow water from the shore, I have been perplexed by the fact that the wreck occurred at all. Even now, having read such source material as I can find, the enigma remains largely unsolved. Nor is it easy to disentangle facts about Forbes's career from legend, for he was one of those men to whom apocryphal tales cling: skilful and resourceful, he was also flamboyant and, at times, undeniably rash. But even at the lowest ebb of his fortunes, when many of his wrecked passengers were castigating him in Melbourne, there were numbers of men ready to defend him. His feats at sea had given him an aura of invincibility that seems to have overawed the colonial authorities.

Maury, Towson, the shipbuilder Donald McKay, and masters like Forbes brought the golden age of sail in answer to gold-hungry emigrants. Records were set by Forbes that were not broken until the days of steam were well advanced.

Forbes was born in Aberdeen in 1821, son of a distinguished advocate there. As a boy he attended the navigation school of a Mr Milne in his home city. According to the Register of Seamen, he went to sea as an apprentice at the age of twelve and for several years was on runs between Aberdeen and the ports of Canada. At twenty-four he became a mate. The Register's description of him then reads: "Complexion—ruddy; Hair—brown; Eyes—blue." He had a scar from a cut over his right eye. His height was only five feet six and three quarter inches.

On 11th August 1852 Forbes received his certificate as master, and his first command appears to have been of Brown and Martin's 1129-ton *Wilson Kennedy* sailing from Quebec to Liverpool that year. Years later the Liverpool *Mercury* said of him: "His rapid passages became a matter of wonderment among the maritime community of the North. While still a young man, Captain Forbes was induced to come to Liverpool and engage in the trade between this port and North America. He was also eminently successful in his new venture, making extraordinarily fast trips, and his fame in this respect commended him to the attention of ship owners and merchants who at that time were deeply interested in establishing great lines of traders between Liverpool and the Australian ports."

One of the shipowners who noticed "Aberdeen" Forbes, as he was then called, was James Baines, a man only a few years his senior, who with Thomas Miller Mackay and others was establishing a line destined to become famous: the Black Ball Line of Australian packets. Baines tried Forbes out on the 421-ton *Cleopatra* and the 1014-ton *Maria*, both on the Liverpool–London run. It is known that he again became noted for fast passages, but what is not known is when and in what capacity he made his first passage to Australia.

Baines, main partner in the firm, was very much a man for the hour. Born in Liverpool—his mother kept a cake shop there—he is reputed to have begun his career by purchasing a dilapidated ship and reaping a handsome profit with her on the run to Australia—this at the time when owners could get away with substandard ships. At the peak of his career, in 1860, the Black Ball Line was to own eighty-six ships and employ some three thousand seamen and three hundred officers. One wonders now what the price was in deaths through sickness and drownings.

Basil Lubbock, noted authority on sailing ships, has described Baines as "a lively, little man, fair with reddish hair. His vitality was abnormal and he had an enthusiastic flow of talk." The intensity of the man shows in the surviving photograph of him. Unfortunately no known photograph has survived of his friend James Forbes, but his signature (see illustration) suggests a man of resolute, flamboyant nature. Forbes gained his experience at sea when loss of life excited little comment and comfort scarcely existed.

In 1851 James Baines ordered Smith and Company of St John, New Brunswick, to construct for him the large clipper ship *Marco Polo*, which was in part his own design. In the opinion of another sailing ship authority, "Warren Armstrong" (William Edward Bennett), this was the "first real clipper ship constructed for the Australian trade; of 1,622 tons registered, she measured 185 feet in length, with a beam of 38 feet and 30 feet depth . . . with three decks, painted ports and a full-length figurehead of the explorer whose name she bore, with ample accommodation for saloon, cabin and steerage passengers, the *Marco Polo* was a vast improvement on anything previously engaged on the Australian run." Shares in her were held by Baines (24), Thomas Harrison (24) and Thomas Miller Mackay (16). She was fitted in the taste of the era: ". . . the dining saloon . . . ceiled with maple and the pilasters . . . panelled with richly ornamented and silvered glass". Between each pilaster was a sheet of plate glass "with cleverly painted, picturesque views . . . with a framework of foliage and scroll in opaque colour and gold". A contrast, for the saloon passengers at least, with the ships of the past.

Baines appointed Forbes master of the *Marco Polo*, heading

a crew of sixty-nine officers and men. At a *déjeuner* held on board her before her departure, he expressed great confidence in both man and ship.

I rise with great diffidence to return you my best thanks for having this day honoured myself and co-owners of the *Marco Polo* with your company, and I may perhaps be excused in feeling some degree of pride in being one of the principal owners of this, the largest vessel, and carrying the greatest number of passengers ever chartered by Government or despatched to Australia with passengers. That we shall endeavour to carry out our contracts with the Commissioners with satisfaction and with credit to ourselves, I think I need not say, in which I am sure we shall be aided to the greatest extent by my friend Captain Forbes, and all the officers of the ship, and I am much mistaken if the *Marco Polo* does not earn for herself a reputation for speed that, when on her return she takes her place as one of the Black Ball Line, she will receive for herself a bumper.

Captain Forbes spoke after Baines. According to Lubbock, Forbes judged from the appearance of the ship that "she could be obliged to go . . . they must not be surprised if they found the *Marco Polo* in the River Mersey that day six months". This must have sounded a rash claim, indeed almost absurd. But Baines had brought about a marriage of master and ship that was to make history.

But while Baines and Forbes and the merchants of Liverpool and their ladies attended the *déjeuner* in sumptuous surroundings, 930 government-sponsored emigrants waited to go aboard. This was well in excess of the number the ship was permitted to carry, even allowing for the fact that children—and there was a large number of them—did not count as full "statute passengers".

Some idea of conditions for the bulk of passengers, both as they waited and during the voyage, can be gained from reports presented to the Victorian Government by Childers and Grimes. They were held at an emigration depot at Birkenhead through which there had been a constant stream of families bound for the colonies and America. Attention to hygiene there had been badly neglected. The children of one *Marco Polo* family had to sleep in a bed vacated that morning by children suffering from a complication of measles. Nine days after the ship sailed, they too were to have measles, which began to spread alarmingly among other steerage families. Childers's report was to disclose that "the after part of the upper deck, which was only five feet in height, had not been originally intended to carry passengers, and under the 15th clause of the Passenger Act could not legally carry them, but was fitted up and occupied at the last moment by direction of the emigration officer at Liverpool". He did not blame Captain Forbes for this; in fact, Edward Grimes was to praise both Forbes and his surgeon-superintendent: "The conduct of the master [was] in every respect good." But he continued: "From statements in the Surgeon's Journal, it appears that when the ship was despatched from Liverpool, the decks are reported to have been lumbered with luggage, and Captain Patey, emigration officer, to have said 'that it could not be avoided, and that the trunks should remain between decks until there was room in the hold.' "

Legally the *Marco Polo* was permitted to carry 701 statute emigrants; she departed with 749½.

7
FIRST VOYAGES OF THE MARCO POLO

Although the records have revealed no earlier voyages to Australia by Captain Forbes, it is scarcely to be believed that he would be appointed master of such a vessel as the *Marco Polo* without having made one in some position of responsibility. He sailed on 4th July 1852. Lubbock, in his *Colonial Clippers*, comments that the emigrants who left with Forbes "were selected with care and reported to be nearly all young and active Britishers". Six hundred and sixty-one of them were Scots, most of them travelling as families.

The voyage out took only sixty-eight days,* a truly astonishing passage, easily beating the auxiliary *Australia* which was claimed to be the fastest ship on the run. The best day's sailing was 364 miles; in four days the average was 336 miles. But on most days infant bodies were slipped into the loneliest of oceans while the ship raced on.

The Melbourne *Argus* of 21st September hailed the *Marco Polo*'s arrival enthusiastically: "This ship has made the quickest passage that any sailing vessel has ever made to this port." She was the largest merchant vessel that had ever visited Australia. In the prevailing excitement, her death toll did not seem untoward: "Fifty-three deaths occurred on board, out of which there are only 2 adults." The fifty-one, not yet being independent, able-bodied men and women, were evidently considered no great loss. The anguish of parents— one couple had lost all five of their children—was not remarked.

* Astonishing though the record was, it was excelled in 1854 by another Black Ball clipper, the *James Baines*, which reduced it to 63 days.

In Hobson's Bay Forbes found scores of ships immobilized, their crews having deserted to make for the diggings. Both Lubbock and Warren Armstrong have it that Forbes charged all his crew with insubordination and had them confined to ship. Not a word of such drastic action appeared in the Melbourne press; in fact the *Argus* mentioned on 6th October that the *Marco Polo*'s captain "J. N. Forbes . . . is spoken of in high terms, both as a gentleman and a commander, by those who have had opportunity of making his acquaintance, since he has been among us".

"Charged with insubordination" is probably an exaggeration. Detective Christie, well known in Melbourne at that time, describes the usual conditions prevailing on ships awaiting turn-around: ". . . in order to prevent the men slipping ashore, great vigilance would have to be exercised by the officers of the ship. The vessel would be out in the bay at anchor, and no person would be allowed on board without their permission, and no seaman who could not be trusted to return, would be allowed to go ashore." No doubt vigilance was at its highest during the gold fever.

On 9th October 1852 the *Marco Polo* sailed. As no telegraph yet existed in Australia, there was no way in which those waiting in England could learn of her departure—unless an outgoing ship in Port Phillip Bay had sighted her and then reached Liverpool before her. But this did not happen, for Forbes was back in the Mersey in seventy-six days, well within the six months he had predicted. Baines, for all his expectations, thought she must have put back through trouble encountered outwardbound. Forbes had in his keeping a 340-ounce nugget of gold, a gift for the Queen from the Government of the new state of Victoria. Its value would scarcely have been commensurate with the Black Ball profits for the voyage.

The *Liverpool Albion* of 3rd January 1853 declared this round passage "the most extraordinary voyage ever recorded". It went on:

. . . on 18th September she cast anchor inside the Port Phillip Heads, thus having made the outward passage in the remarkably brief space of

68 days, a passage never even approached, excepting by the ship *Statesman*, which made the run from Plymouth in 76 days. . . . Captain Forbes lately commanded the ships *Maria* and *Cleopatra* belonging to the same firm. His passages in the *Cleopatra** were little less surprising than the present voyage. Though comparatively a young man, Captain Forbes's abilities as a navigator are of the first order. His voyage to the antipodes was made on the great circle system.

Forbes's name was made. People came from all over England to see the *Marco Polo*. On 13th March 1853 he sailed in her again for Melbourne, this time with 648 passengers. Lubbock has it that Forbes was in "a very confident mood, and, as soon as the ship was under weigh, had his passengers called together to address them. 'Ladies and gentlemen, last trip I astonished the world with the sailing of this ship. This trip I intend to astonish God Almighty.' "

Although the words do not sound out of character, it is doubted by some authorities that Forbes ever spoke them. Lubbock tends at times to be drawn to the colourful; nevertheless another of his claims can be supported by eye-witness evidence: "Captain Forbes was a very lithe, active man," Lubbock relates, "and one day, as the result of a challenge, he crawled hand over hand from the spanker boom end to the shark's fin on the jibboom, not such a difficult feat, though not a usual one for the master of a ship." Later, "whilst on the *Lightning*, it was his custom to go out on the swinging boom when the lower stunsail was set and to calmly survey his ship from the boom end, when she was tearing along before the westerlies."

The second voyage of the *Marco Polo* was not so fast. On 8th April on his outward voyage, Forbes wrote to Baines from latitude 1° 30′ north, longitude 20° 30′ west:

DEAR SIR,

We have got so far on towards our destination. We have had nothing but calms and adverse winds since we left Liverpool. We have boarded several vessels from London, with passengers, but my passengers say they would rather be on the *Marco Polo* than any of them. My passage

---

* Although Forbes had once commanded the *Cleopatra*, the records do not show her as having been under his command on the Australian run.

33

will be made when I get South of the Line, which I expect will be tomorrow. I will get wind, which I have not had North of the Line. We have had one death, a child seven months old, and one birth, which makes our number good. I have got about 40 of the expertest thieves on board from London and, which is worse, two or three of them are in the first cabin. I will only add that I have not had one word of complaint against ship, provisions, master or officers, which is a great thing to say, and they are all going to write home to their friends to come out in your new ship.* Last voyage we had 20 deaths before these number of days out, but then we were under government orders. . . .

JAMES FORBES

His last quoted comment needs expanding. Ships chartered by the British government usually carried large numbers of families; among the children the death-rate was often high. Emigrant ships leaving independently, on the other hand, usually carried a predominance of young men, much better able to withstand the rigours of the journey. Hence the marked difference in loss of life. From reading Forbes' letter to Baines one would suppose the writer to be an amiable, restrained man. A vastly different individual gradually emerges from the diary of one of his Melbourne-bound passengers, William Culshaw Greenhalgh. On March 17th, the fourth day out, Greenhalgh wrote: "At 9.30 p.m. the Captain came to see the lights extinguished, made several complaints, spoke his mind pretty freely, did not forget to say who he was, ordered no card playing after 8 p.m. and swore he (would) put the first man in irons that disobeyed his orders."

On March 23rd, when Captain Forbes was again doing his evening rounds, he "caught one of the Stewards carrying a bottle of spirits for some passengers on deck after hours, for which the captain got enraged, struck him several times and afterwards abused him shamefully by striking him with a large glass ship's lamp, cutting his face in several places, breaking his nose and giving him a pair of black eyes." The man was unable to work next day.

On April 22nd "a man was put in irons for being drunk and insulting the first mate. (He) was for several days fed upon

* The *Lightning*, then in the course of construction at Boston, U.S.A.

bread and water. He would not be silent, so the captain, who was determined not to have his noise, ordered him to be gagged, which consisted of a piece of rusty iron (being) placed in his mouth and tied behind his head. A very painful operation, soon fetched blood; was in this state for an hour and then allowed to have it out."

Another side of Forbes' make-up is shown in an entry made on May 6th. The crew were exhausted after stormy weather and passengers were helping to reef sails. The captain was also "in the rigging reefing sails". But there were soon afterwards blows and irons and bread and water for other crew members. Far south, in violent weather, one of the sailors placed in irons "was so starved and frozen, he could not move his hands. The mate afterwards struck him and jumped upon him. . . . . The captain asked him if he would submit. He would not answer and he ordered him to remain in irons and be fed on bread and water".

It seems evident that Forbes, perhaps with the knowledge of his company, cheated some of his Melbourne-bound passengers. The destination shown on the tickets of some was "Port Phillip". In Liverpool they had been assured that this was, to all intents and purposes, the same as showing "Melbourne", but during the voyage Forbes declared that these people must pay him ten shillings a head if they wished to be landed in Melbourne. "(It) is a very nice thing for him," wrote Greenhalgh. "Of course we can do nothing because we are in his hands and if we don't pay him ten shillings, it would cost us more. . . . It is the general opinion that the whole company are are a complete lot of rogues."

Approaching the western entrance to Bass Strait the *Marco Polo* encountered "heavy sea . . . hail and snow; most of the ropes frozen with ice. . . . The captain in a frightful rage, cursing and swearing at the sailors." Not for five days was he able to take observations of the sun. On the sixth day they sighted Cape Otway.

Although her second voyage was not as fast as the first, the *Marco Polo* was back in the Mersey in exactly six months, this time with £280,000 of gold dust. By now Forbes's reputation was soaring.

8
THE LIGHTNING

Baines now sent Forbes to Boston to superintend the fitting out of a new Black Ball clipper, the *Lightning*, one of Donald McKay's ships. The ship was 243 feet long and 44 feet in beam, its mainmast 164 feet high with a beam yard 90 feet long; she carried 13,000 square yards of canvas.

Favourable comment appeared in the Boston *Daily Atlas* marking Forbes's acceptance of the new ship: "Captain James Nicol Forbes, being a pious man, was attended down the harbour by a select party of brethren and sisters of the church, who, at parting, gave him their best wishes and their blessing. This is much better than the dram-drinking and vociferous cheering which usually make up the parting scenes of the unregenerated."

Arriving in Liverpool after her delivery voyage, she was acclaimed the fastest ship in the world, having covered 436 miles in twenty-four hours, a distance not matched by steam-ships for thirty years.* (It is of interest to compare this with the best days' runs by the famous 150-ton schooner *America*, sailing the Atlantic under Captain Dick Brown in July 1851 and destined to carry off the One Hundred Guineas Cup around the Isle of Wight: 284, 276, and 254 miles.)

The *Lightning* departed from Liverpool for Melbourne on 14th May 1854. On the outward voyage a twenty-nine-year-old merchant, John Fenwick, kept a journal, and from it clear pictures emerge of "Bully" Forbes and the travelling con-

* The ultimate record in sail, 465 nautical miles in a day, was set later by another Black Ball clipper, *Champion of the Seas*.

ditions of the time. Early on the voyage Fenwick wrote, "The Captain says we must set every yard of canvas, and if that does not make her go, we must put up our Shirts. It is amusing to observe his anxious watchfulness—every step or two he looks up at the sails and whistles for a wind. Then he orders a pull at this and a stretch at that. But to see him seriously whistling—that's the joke."

On this voyage the captain's sister travelled with him. Mr and Mrs Fenwick appear to have seen a good deal of the brother and sister during the voyage and to have been accorded favoured treatment.

On the night of 9th June, a night of full moon and strong winds, the *Lightning* was far south in the Atlantic.

There was letting go and easing off for a few minutes—the Captain had then come on deck and we were nearly on our side (i.e. the ship). "Let go the Jibs." "The Jib Boom is overboard, Sir!" was the cool reply from the Boatswain forward—it went the same instant the order was given. The Capt. was on the forecastle in a moment and in another he was overboard with a rope to secure the wreck. . . . What a roaring of wind, a thundering of flapping sails, dashing of spray, shrieking of orders there were before we were anyway snug again.

This incident certainly lends credence to Lubbock's claim that Forbes would climb hand over hand out the spanker boom. Next day a fellow cabin passenger remarked to Fenwick, "We ought to petition the Captain to keep up less sail, for he sees very little difference between frightening a man out of his wits and killing him outright."

On 13th June the *Lightning* ran perilously close to some remote islands; the sea changed from "deep Blue to a fine pea green. I remarked to the Captain that there could not be very much water there. 'Oh! yes,' said he, 'we have 7 fathoms—four will do for us!' This is running rather fine—the ship draws 3 fathoms and there was a heavy swell."

On 16th July the passengers received a shock that must have left them with little desire ever to travel again by sea.

The Captain expecting to sight Kerguelen's Land during the night, the watch had to keep a good look out. Abt 10, it was said we were only abt

60 miles off the Islands. Abt 11, the Fore top Stunsail Boom was carried away and almost immediately after LAND AHEAD was echoed along the poop. The carrying away of the Boom had brought the Captain on deck, so that that misfortune proved our Salvation. The land might be 1 or 2 miles off. The Helm was put up and the ship fell off, and by the time I was dressed and on deck we were coasting along—the land being to Windward of us. Hardly had we been assured that we were out of danger, when "LAND AHEAD AGAIN, SIR!" put us all on the alert. There were a great many prompt orders from the Captain and as quickly executed, for ALL HANDS were up. Again we seemed to be safe, when again, "LAND AHEAD!" and the Boatswain ran to the Captain, "Land on the Lee Bow, sir." "All right," said the Captain, "Hard up the Helm." Again more orders, and I, seeing the sailors alone and the Bulwarks on both sides crowded with people looking, but doing no good, I gave my feeble help to the ropes. Still the "Land ahead" shouting from the Forecastle. "Land on the Port Bow!" A man in the Main chains, sounding and shouting to the Captain. He shouting to the Mate and Bos'un, they again to the men—at last the Crisis appeared inevitable— "Breakers on the Lee Bow!" shouted the Mate., The sailors I was pulling with said, "It's all up now by G—." A great many were on the Forecastle with their Life Belts on—all waited for the shock—there was land on 3 sides of us & no room to turn, the wind blowing right aft. As soon as the Mate gave the last alarming intimation, the Capt. shouted at the pitch of his voice, "Mr. Hodge!" (the Boatswain) 2 or 3 times— no reply. "Pull quietly men & don't sing," said the 2nd Mate to us; a long minute, perhaps more passed—it seemed an age. At last Hodge replied—"ALL RIGHT, Sir." Then, "Let go the Bunt Lines, Haul in the Main Tack—Yo, hoy." "Hurrah—We're clear!" It was news we could not exactly believe at first—in fact, it was not till after we were all clear, that we could exactly feel the danger we had escaped. . . . The Coast was precipitous, rocky & covered with snow, & the night was very dark & very cold. How few could have reached the shore, and even there, How few could have survived on the Desolate & Barren Land in the depth of Winter!

A name to be remembered from this very close call is that of the boatswain, Hodge (correctly Hodges), for he was later boatswain on the *Schomberg* and was called upon to give evidence concerning his captain's lack of action.

After this incident had passed, the captain declared, "It was ridiculous of people to be frightened—'Breakers on both Bows & Breakers under the Bow'—they must imagine we don't know where we are—as if we were on an Exploring expedition—I just came to the place I steered for, and if I had missed it, you would have said I did not know my business.' " But Fenwick observes,

If he wilfully came thro' those Islands & reefs on such a dark night, it was to say the least, *highly imprudent*; a very little mishap would have cost us all our lives—many a ship has been lost in a much better position. Except the Capt. & Mate (whose real opinions we do not know), all the others thought it was a case. The probability, however, is that he merely intended to *sight* the Land in order to confirm his position, & that we were between the islands before he knew it. At anyrate, he deserves some credit for his coolness & promptitude until we were out of the "fix".

Forbes must have sensed Fenwick's doubts, for on 26th July he invited Mr and Mrs Fenwick "into his private cabin when we took wine and saw his charts. He declares that he saw land on the 16th & had his sister on deck looking at it fully $\frac{1}{4}$ hour before the Lookout saw it & before the Stunsail Boom was carried away. He also knew exactly that we would go between the Islands etc. etc. Anyhow, this is his proper policy to be so knowing on the subject, but I don't doubt the less that he found himself unexpectedly between the Islands."

Clearly Fenwick was a man not to be talked out of his own assessment, much as he admired the captain's skill. Undoubtedly the whole incident of the Kerguelen Islands and Forbes's later pooh-poohing of its risks throws light on his make-up. For all his skill, he was riding for a fall.

There is one further entry in Fenwick's journal that has significance when the loss of the *Schomberg* is considered. He states that land was sighted at Cape Bridgewater, a hundred and twenty miles back from Cape Otway. That same evening, at 6 o'clock, they "tacked ship and during the night, a good breeze took us right off the land". A prudent move, since the coast there was poorly charted and Forbes was familiar with its reputation.

Next day, 30th July, Fenwick records, "Gradually coming round to our course. 3 p.m. land on both sides. King's Island on the right & Cape Otway on the left [Note: It would not be possible for both to have been seen.]—blowing very fresh and rainy—a nasty night—a good lookout kept." Forbes was obviously making a careful entry to Bass Strait—a contrast with his later handling of the *Schomberg*.

The voyage had taken seventy-seven days—not fast by Forbes's standards, though he had had four excellent days when the *Lightning* logged 332, 348, 311, and 329 nautical miles. It was reported in the Liverpool *Times* that "during the stay of the *Lightning* in Hobson's Bay she created quite an excitement, and was visited by hundreds of people. On 13th August a *déjeuner* was given on board, which was attended by upwards of one hundred of the principal ladies and gentlemen at Melbourne."

The *Lightning*'s return voyage was an astonishing one and set a Liverpool–Melbourne–Liverpool record never excelled by sailing ships. The Liverpool *Times* reported:

The magnificent clipper-ship *Lightning*, J. N. Forbes, arrived in the Mersey on Monday, after the most remarkable passage ever recorded in the annals of navigation. She left Melbourne on Sunday afternoon, the 20th August, and thus her run here is rather under sixty-three days.

The *Lightning* sailed hence on the 14th May, and has made the voyage out and home, including the detention of twenty clear days at her anchors in Hobson's Bay in 5 months 21 hours. [This] is unprecedently short, notwithstanding that the outward run, from the nature of the winds experienced, occupied longer than might have reasonably been expected from the well-known qualifications of the ship, and the great ability of her commander.

The ship "averaged close upon 300 miles per day. . . . On the 8th September, at 3 a.m., Cape Horn bore N.W. distant 50 miles, being a run of only 19 days mean time from Port Phillip Heads, by far the fastest ever recorded either under canvas or steam." In a little over forty days out from Melbourne she had reached the equator, "an extraordinary achievement, considering the adverse winds encountered after rounding Cape Horn". At the conclusion of a long account of the voyage, the *Times* reported that "the *Lightning* has brought upwards of eighty passengers, and 40,000 ounces of gold dust on freight, besides a large amount in the hands of passengers. She has also brought answers to the letters of the 13th June, making a course of post of only 132 days."

Again apocryphal tales are heard. Lubbock has it that during this record voyage "Forbes carried on in the most daring manner . . . keeping his station at the break of the poop with a pistol in each hand in order to prevent his scared crew from letting go the royal halliards". Neither the Liverpool *Mercury* nor the Liverpool *Times* reports any such happenings; indeed, the *Mercury* relates that "the lady passengers by the *Lightning* have presented Captain Forbes with a handsome silver goblet".

"Bully", or "Aberdeen", Forbes* was now without doubt the most outstanding sailing-ship master of them all.

---

* It has been claimed by some that the appellation "Bully" signified "firstrate" or "goodfellow". While this might have been so, his nature suggests otherwise.

9
THE SCHOMBERG

Captain Forbes was discharged from the *Lightning* in Liverpool on 23rd October 1854. During a spell of about eleven
months ashore he married, but the maiden name of Jane, his
twenty-three-year-old bride, has not so far been traced. It is
probable that Margaret, first child of the marriage, was born
either shortly before or shortly after her father returned to sea.

Forbes was the obvious man for Baines to select for appointment to the new *Schomberg*; moreover, the two men had
become close friends—later Forbes was godfather to Baines's
second daughter, born in 1855.

The Aberdeen-built *Schomberg* was given exultant publicity,
for there had been disappointment both in Britain and
Australia that the record-breaking clippers had so far all been
built in North America. Named after Captain Schomberg,
R.N., the Chief Government Emigration Agent in Liverpool,
she was of 2600 tons, 288 feet long and 29 feet in depth. The
height of her mainmast and her spread of sail are still awe-
inspiring: 210 feet to the maintop and 16,000 square yards—
or 3.3 acres—of sail.

The Melbourne *Argus* reported that the vessel was "built on
the diagonal principle, which is calculated to secure the
greatest strength. Her thickness consists of four courses of
Scotch larch, each $2\frac{1}{2}$ inches thick, and between each is a layer
of hair felt, the outside or skin being of pitch pine, 5 inches
thick—the whole combined by means of patent trenails. . . . She
has three decks." At this point the *Argus* became ecstatic:

"The lower cabin contains sixty large staterooms, finished with white and gold . . . the ladies' cabin or drawing-room is inlaid with rosewood, set off into Grecian arched panels, and ornamented with pilasters, papier mache cornices, gilding and flower work, the windows filled with transparencies." So it went on: doors of bird's-eye maple; a library of four hundred volumes; velvet pile carpets; mahogany furniture; a sofa at the upper end of the drawing room that would seat thirty; chairs covered with damask. Fowls, pigs, and a cow were carried, and the water tanks held 90,000 gallons. There were even some baths.

Altogether, for the extent of accommodation, as well as for the utmost provision being made for the comfort of passengers—we might say the gratification of their tastes—it would be difficult to conceive it possible what more could have been done in the case of a ship. . . . She will carry 1000 passengers with ease and comfort. . . . She is to be commanded by Captain J. Nicol Forbes, an Aberdonian, whose unrivalled voyages in the *Lightning* and *Marco Polo* have given him a world-wide reputation. Captain Forbes . . . has expressed the utmost confidence of being able with the *Schomberg* to eclipse all his former efforts. . . . It is right to mention that this really magnificent vessel . . . is . . . the work of Messrs. Hall. How much credit she does them requires no laudation here—the vessel herself furnishes their best eulogium; and for the rest, deeds, not words, may be left to speak.

Having read this description—which does not appear to have touched on steerage accommodation— James Ballingall, the Melbourne ship surveyor who had fought so long for safer ships, wrote rapturously to the *Argus*: "I added together the thickness of the planks etc. and found that they formed a solid body of wood fifteen inches thick, besides the felt, in the bottom and sides throughout the length and breadth of the ship. . . . Having advocated the subject of solid bottoms and sides to merchant vessels . . . for five-and-twenty years past, I feel grateful to the Almighty for having been permitted to see the adoption of them." From the Black Ball Line Mr Ballingall had learnt that they hoped the *Schomberg* would "reach your port in about sixty days".

The departure was advertised in the Liverpool *Daily Post*:

THE SPLENDID NEW CLIPPER SHIP
SCHOMBERG
J. N. FORBES, COMMANDER,
celebrated for his wonderful passages in the MARCO POLO and
LIGHTNING . . . is expected she will prove herself the fastest ship in
the world . . .

Daring words; a daring master!

Larger ship though the *Schomberg* was than Forbes's other
commands, she was carrying on departure only about a third
of the passengers that the *Marco Polo* had carried on her
first, overcrowded voyage. No doubt this was attributable to
the efforts made in Melbourne to cut loadings down to 350
passengers. She carried approximately 320. The exact number
is confused by the fact that in three cases number of children in
a family and number of servants are not given. Her cargo was
chiefly "iron and plant"—including two thousand tons of
railway lines—for the Melbourne–Geelong railway. She was
reputedly insured for £300,000.

Lubbock claims that before departure "Forbes was too
ready with wine-tinted promises of what he would do with the
Schomberg" and that "on 6th October, 1855, she was hauled
through the pier heads amidst the cheers of a patriotic crowd
of sightseers, with the boast of 'Sixty days to Melbourne' flying
from her signal halliards". And there is the oft-repeated boast
attributed to Forbes: "Hell or Melbourne in sixty days." Even
though these reports *sound* like Forbes and might well be true,
other authorities have doubted them.

It was customary for a representative of the Liverpool
Seamen's and Emigrants' Friend Society and Bethel Union to
hold a final service on departing emigrant ships. James Buck
officiated on the *Schomberg*. Although full of eulogies for the
ship, his message to the passengers was stern. "Their need of
mercy as sinners condemned and unworthy and liable to
perish, was clearly pointed out, and their peculiar circumstances as strangers in a strange land, and as intending voyagers
over the mighty deep, where dangers in a thousand trying
forms might await them . . .." Small wonder that many "were
overcome by their feelings", but at least Mr Buck was able to

go ashore consoling himself that, "if I never see them again, I feel I am clear from responsibility . . . ."

The last mails were brought out by steamer at 9 p.m. All told, the ship now carried 17,093 letters and 31,800 newspapers for Australia. Mr Buck continues, "Commodore Forbes, commander of the ship, and his lady, and other friends, with myself, entered the steamer, and, as we pushed off three loud cheers broke forth from the noble vessel. . . . The next morning (Saturday) her anchor was weighed, and by eight o'clock she was outside the river, her voyage having commenced."

Jane Forbes was then twenty-four. Lonely though she must have felt, she could scarcely have been other than a proud wife.

10
THE FATAL VOYAGE

From the outset the *Schomberg* was beset by calms or, at best, light winds. According to an unidentified passenger quoted in the Melbourne *Argus*, she was becalmed for ten days while still six degrees north of the equator, then, "in consequence of the Trades being southerly they were forced to hug within five miles of the South American coast, south of Pernambuco. They then intended to land at Tristan d'Acuna for fresh provisions, but the wind again calmed, and they lost nearly a week." This passenger believed the ship to have been over-loaded, but no such allegation was raised at the subsequent inquiries.

The delays must have been galling for Forbes, though the unknown passenger reported that he "conducted himself as a thorough seaman, and was always up, night and day, when in the neighbourhood of land".

Probably the most dependable outline of the voyage until the time the Australian coast was sighted is contained in an explanatory letter written by Forbes himself and published in the Melbourne *Argus* of 4th January 1856:

The royal mail-ship *Schomberg*, sailed from Liverpool on the 6th October, and in the early part of the voyage met with light baffling winds, the equator not being crossed until the 28th day after sailing, and a detention of ten days from calms marking the crossing of the Line. From the equator to the meridian of Greenwich the ship met with light, baffling, and contrary winds, which protracted the voyage to fifty-five days from our departure from Liverpool—the distance ordinarily occupying not more than thirty-eight days. From this date until our arrival at 150° east longitude, we encountered fine steady breezes and her greatest speed during the distance being 15½ knots per hour. From this date, 22nd December, met with adverse winds from east to east-south-east, blowing fresh. On Christmas Day first made land at Cape Bridgewater, about one o'clock p.m. . . . .

He was now eighty days out from England.

There is no reason to doubt this account; in fact, it is noteworthy that Captain Forbes made his landfall at the same point as he had done on the *Lightning* voyage described by Fenwick. This suggests that he had a deliberate procedure. A landfall one hundred and twenty miles west of Cape Otway was a good one, provided the master then stood safely out to sea and headed approximately south-east. Nearly all the coast within fifty miles of Cape Otway was a battlement of cliffs.

Between the Christmas Day landfall and loss of the ship on Boxing Day, it is difficult to afford credence to Forbes's account, especially when it is borne in mind that he was not on deck during the most critical period of those two days. More convincing are the words of his boatswain, James Hodges, who, though no navigator and much discredited in court, had been sailing four years with Forbes and obviously knew a great deal about ship-handling in situations close to dangerous shores. These words of his are taken from the final inquiry in Melbourne:

I should think we were then [at Cape Bridgewater] within about a quarter of a mile of the coast. The coast is almost perpendicular there. We were so close that we could see the breakers quite plain. We put the ship about then, stood out to the westward, and lost sight of the coast. ["Westward" was incorrect, as to stand away from land would be to move *southward*. This error will be referred to later.] We stood in again towards the land about the middle of the day. We made the land again in the evening. We were going on a wind, and the ship was braced sharp up. On the first occasion when we sighted land I was called upon deck by the seamen, and I took upon myself to pipe all hands and put about the ship without orders. When I saw land on the second time, it was between ten and eleven o'clock at night. I was called to pipe all hands to put the ship about. I could see land quite plain at that time. It was a fine night. It was very light, but I think the moon was clouded. It was about twenty minutes before the ship was put about. She was close-hauled on the starboard tack. She was going towards shore. Before the word was given to put the ship about I saw breakers on the lee side, a mile or two distant. I saw the breakers twenty minutes before the ship was put about. Just as I came on deck I spoke to Captain Forbes and asked him if he saw the reef. He said, "Yes". The order was not then given to put the ship about. The hands were all waiting for orders. . . . When the orders were given to put the helm down, the ship came head to wind, and when they came to haul the main yard she began to pay off and missed stays. She went to the left instead of the right. The after yards were then squared to wear ship, and bring her on the other tack. She began to pay off before the wind, but could not clear the point. She went aground bows foremost on a sandy rock, as I believe.

As casually as this was the great ship brought to destruction and her captain's reputation ruined. The manoeuvres described suggest that the *Schomberg* was stranded about three hundred yards from shore on the sandy spit that ends in a low rock stack—the most prominent feature of what is now known as the Schomberg Reef—her bows toward the present town of Peterborough, a town that did not exist at the time of the wreck.

Hodges's statement contains the further extraordinary words: "The Captain was on deck, and he remained on deck up to the time the ship was lost." One is baffled to find so competent a master standing twenty minutes without taking action to save his ship. It would have been better had he not been there; had Hodges been free to take it upon himself again to "put about ship without orders".

Tragic though the situation was for Forbes and his ship, it was also ludicrous. The great *Schomberg* had almost beached herself. How she reached the sand spit without running onto one of the numerous rock stacks farther to the west is beyond understanding. And how did she come to be in the locality at all? Her proper track should have taken her ten miles off the coast at that point. Forbes had certainly not followed his *Lightning* procedure of standing well off until he had sighted the Otway light. Intentionally or unintentionally he had coasted along a shore known to be dangerous and imperfectly charted, so close in that the light would certainly have been screened by the bulk of Moonlight Head.

Forbes's reputation might have suffered less could he have perished with his ship; it was a jibe of fate that his life was perfectly safe. A well-known Melbourne engineer, John F. Millar, who was among the passengers, took charge of a boat to seek out a landing place. Unaccountably he could not find one, though the high dunes thereabouts must have been clearly visible. As the sea was relatively calm, Forbes and all those for whom he was responsible were in little danger; they could have waded most of the distance ashore. The *Schomberg* had drifted into one of the only beaches along that part of the coast. A mile or so farther east might well have meant complete loss of life, for the cliffs there cannot be scaled and the tide reaches to their base.

Forbes had "rockets and blue lights . . . let off and guns fired in case any sail might be in sight". They were fortunately sighted by the coastal steamer *Queen*. Warrnambool, thirty miles westward, was the nearest town of any size. According to the *Warrnambool Examiner* news was brought there by "the successive arrivals of the *Queen* and the *Champion*. A short time after [the wreck] the *Queen* steamer was seen in the distance on her way to Warrnambool, and Captain Doran at once bore up to the wreck, and, without loss of time, nearly all passengers and the mails were transferred to the steamer without any mishap."

It rather bears out the lack of real danger that a passenger, Joseph Wilkie, claimed later that "Captain Forbes could easily have landed us all in safety on the beach and with less labor to his men than putting us on the *Queen*".

Though the weather was fine, the new land must have looked inhospitable indeed to the immigrants as dawn broke. There was only one small hut to be seen by a wide river estuary. Most of them went on to Melbourne with few if any possessions. Three days later a gale blew up. When it had done with the *Schomberg*, there was no hope of her being refloated and repaired. The *Warrnambool Examiner* reported that "the sea was making a clean breach over her, and as the vessel was continually twisting about, her seams opening, there can be no doubt she will be totally destroyed. There was a fearful surf on yesterday which would soon hasten the work of destruction." On that Saturday Captain Forbes abandoned the ship. He sailed to Melbourne with Mr Shillinglaw of the Water Police and various other officials—an altogether humiliating arrival for an idolized man.

As for "the noblest ship that ever floated on the water", boats were capsized in attempts to reach her, but passengers' luggage—or some of it—was retrieved. She was quickly becoming a total loss. "As the wreck covers a coast line of four miles," said the *Examiner*, "we understand many 'wreckers' are on the look out." Messrs MacDonald and Lascellers auctioned whatever remained. Spirits, butter, and the ship's boats seem to have been the main items to fetch reasonable prices. "The remainder of the wreck, cargo, and stores, whether in the sea, on the beach, or wherever else found was purchased by Messrs. Manifold & Bostock for £65."

So much for all her luxuries. Even at that, the wreckers seem to have profited most; they came "with drays, and other means of carrying away booty". For weeks afterwards, local Aborigines were seen wearing dresses in ways never envisaged in London fashion houses.

A bizarre touch in the local scene was the arrival in Warrnambool on 4th January of "the crew of the *Schomberg* ... preceded by the fine band of the ill-fated vessel. The men had walked the whole distance from the wreck." By 7th January only the bowsprit and a portion of the forepart of the vessel were discernible, and she was expected soon to break up entirely. In fact, the hull, or the bulk of it, remained intact, and nine years after the wreck two sea captains and a Melbourne merchant purchased it. But the *Argus* of 10th September 1864 reported a telegram from Port Fairy (or Belfast as it then was) telling of their fate: "News has just been received that Mr. Hall and Captain Seely of Melbourne have been drowned from a small boat while engaged in searching for the wreck of the *Schomberg*." This suggests that in the weather conditions prevailing it was difficult for them to so much as locate their purchase, or possibly they were not familiar with the area. At all events, a second salvage attempt was made in the following year. Local tradition has it that the hull was towed from the Schomberg Reef, but that the towlines broke before much progress was made. This tradition was lent support 116 years later when the submerged hull was re-located, as the Epilogue will relate.

In contrast with some of the other wrecks along the Otway coast, loss of the *Schomberg* had been a relatively tame business—there had been no pitting of a determined master against great odds; no heroic acts or loss of life. But the ship had been the pride of Britain and her master the most highly regarded of all captains. Inevitably there were serious repercussions for Forbes. It is reasonable to assume that had such a stranding occurred in Britain, his career would have ended in ignominy. He was fortunate that in the infant colony the inquiries were bungled.

11
THE PROTEST MEETING

The Chamber of Commerce in Melbourne had formed a relief committee as soon as the implications of the wreck were realized. "There were some cases of mothers and children who were altogether destitute, the husbands being at the diggings." Accounts of the wreck were strangely conflicting, nor were they clarified by a protest meeting held on 4th January in the Melbourne Mechanics Institution; indeed, to the reader 120 years later, the tone of the meeting is baffling.

"The CHAIRMAN declared that the meeting had been called for the purpose of investigating the cause of the wreck and reclaiming the luggage of the passengers." The resolutions passed soon proved the gathering completely incompetent to investigate causes even had this been its proper function. The first resolution was "that the conduct of the captain, the surgeon, and officers of the *Schomberg* was ungentlemanly, discourteous, and tyrannical, and grossly immoral".

Tyranny and immorality, especially immorality, were uppermost in the minds of the passengers. As an example of tyranny: "The Captain entered Mr. Melville's cabin, and the latter gentleman complained that . . . provisions were of quality not fit for a dog. To this the captain replied that they were a set of dirty dogs, and what they had was good enough. (Hisses)." Again, "He had taken two unfortunate Irishmen out of their berths in the night, and confined them in the wheelhouse until four or five o'clock in the morning. He called them at the same time, 'a d—d Irish crew and set of rebels'. . . . Had he said so much to an Irishman ashore he would have had his physiognomy disfigured. (Cheers)."

It sounds in character with Forbes, but completely irrelevant to the loss of the ship. When the passengers turned to the matter of immorality, their virtuous indignation knew no bounds.

There were two "lady" passengers on board in the 2nd cabin. . . . These females were kept out of their cabins by the captain and his officers until very unseasonable hours. The first occasion on which any dispute arose on the matter was when one of these ladies was kept in the captain's cabin until one o'clock in the morning. The second lady preferred the daylight, for she came back at four in the morning and then only in her night-dress. ("Oh!" and "Shame!"). The door of her cabin, however, was shut against her, and she did not obtain entrance until a full exposure of her conduct had been made.

"It was a notorious fact," declared another passenger, "that the captain of the *Schomberg* kept a woman in the second cabin. (Great laughter). And the same thing with the doctor; it was every day, all day, and all night. (Uproarious laughter). When he went to the doctor for some medicine he saw this female sitting in his cabin. A PASSENGER: I have seen her in the bed. (Laughter). It was on St. Stephen's day. (Great laughter)."

These were passengers who had not long survived shipwreck in a strange land, who might have been expected to have more on their minds than a wish to expose, with such evident relish, the captain's alleged moral lapses. Such, though, was the climate of the times. I recall my own grandmother telling me in her nineties that "Bully" Forbes had been below deck "playing cards with lady friends" when the emergency arose. Her tone left me in no doubt that they were not "ladies". This seemed more reprehensible to her than his absence from the deck.

Then there were complaints at the meeting about the food—"they killed the pigs after they died"—and some believable comments on the captain's rashness: when they had approached another ship in the Southern Ocean, "he, without any specific purpose, ran so close that he carried away the signal haulyards", and again, when they had sighted an iceberg, he "ran the vessel so close that . . . the keel must have gone over a portion of it".

The single conclusion of any worth to come from this

extraordinary meeting was "that the loss of that fine ship can only be attributed to the gross negligence of the captain".

Next day the *Argus* carried a strong leading article:

. . . To the arrival of this vessel everyone who takes an interest in shipping matters had long been looking, and even national pride was concerned in the desire to have it demonstrated that all fast clippers are not built by Donald McKay. In a country like this, wherein nine-tenths of the population at least possess the amount of nautical experience conferred by a voyage half round the world, the *Schomberg*, from the first moment when we heard of the laying of her keel to that at which we were startled by the sudden news of her destruction, has occupied an amount of public attention . . . that would very likely seem unaccountable in most other places.

The disappointment and regret felt at the loss of a ship on which such great expectations had been centred has subsequently been much increased by widespread rumors varying as to the culpability imputed, but the mildest of them charging Captain Forbes with improper conduct as the ruler on board a passenger ship, and great carelessness as to the safety of his vessel. Other opinions have been freely expressed, not merely at yesterday's meeting, but elsewhere, that the *Schomberg* was intentionally wrecked. Of the latter offence we do not believe Captain Forbes to have been guilty, but even with respect to this matter there are such grounds for suspicion as to render strict inquiry most desirable, for Captain Forbes's sake, if he be innocent—for the sake of society in any case. In such cases as this we are not inclined to be contented with the verdict of such a meeting as that of yesterday. The passengers of a wrecked ship constitute the proper witnesses, but the wrong jury, when the captain is upon his trial.

But the *Argus* went on to point out that there was "no regularly-constituted tribunal before which the causes of a shipwreck can be made the subject of investigation. Sometimes the captain, if he feels that the foregone conclusions of the public do him injustice, may indeed court inquiry, but if he feels that it is better to be suspended than convicted, it is exceedingly difficult to bring him to proper account. Thus the present system gives that man most chances of immunity when he knows himself most to deserve punishment."

Unfortunately, no marine board of inquiry yet existed. There were proper channels for investigating wreck of British ships in foreign waters and for ships of the Royal Navy wherever they might be wrecked, but none for British passenger ships wrecked in colonial waters. As a result of this, three highly unsatisfactory hearings were held.

In the meantime, Captain Forbes wrote to the *Argus* defending himself: "Sir, I avail myself of the earliest opportunity afforded me since the melancholy catastrophe of the loss of the royal mail-ship *Schomberg*, under my command, to communicate to the public of the Australian colonies the information regarding the voyage and final loss of that magnificent ship, which they are justly entitled to demand and I am equally anxious to furnish." He then described the outward journey as already quoted, but concluded it with an unconvincing account of the actual wreck. There could be no explaining away his proximity to such a notorious shore.

12
FIRST AND SECOND INQUIRIES

The first formal hearing took place at Williamstown court on 17th January before Lieutenant Pasco, R.N. The charges were laid by "Mr. Broad, Immigration Agent, at the instance of several of the passengers . . . against Captain Forbes for a breach of the Passenger Act of 1855". Again one is bewildered at the turn of events: a report running to three newspaper columns deals only with the poor quality of food provided, not with the poor approach to Bass Strait. The case continued next day with Forbes's lawyer, Albert Read, astutely playing off the complaints of some passengers about food against the satisfaction of others. He tied the unorganized passengers in knots and was even able to declare that "the charge was no more than a burlesque on the loss of so noble a ship. The passengers ought to be thankful to Captain Forbes for saving their lives." The charges were dismissed.

On 22nd January Forbes was recalled to Williamstown to face the more serious charge of "neglect of duty", laid by Mr Shillinglaw of the Water Police. This was heard by Lieutenant Pasco (chairman), Captain Ferguson (Harbour Master) and Lieutenant Crawford, R.N. Forbes's counsel, Mr Read, again carried the day by successfully confining the accusation to one alleged omission: Forbes's failure to let the anchor go at the proper time. How the *Schomberg* came to be where she was, was again not mentioned. Indeed, Read claimed this time that Forbes's "experienced eye" detected that what the third officer had thought was a fog-bank was in fact land. "What did he do? Why, with cool judgement he ordered all hands out ready to put the ship about. . . . The Captain thought he was safe then, when he had got the ship round, and what prevented him from being safe? Why, a hidden sandbank not marked in any chart with which their Worships, as experienced men, were acquainted." The charges were dismissed, but Forbes was called to appear at the next court of Criminal Sessions before the Chief Justice.

13
CRIMINAL
PROCEEDINGS

The Crown Solicitor, Robert Molesworth, had by now gathered damning evidence from passengers and lower deck crew. (It was not considered proper to seek evidence from Forbes's officers.) Arthur Melville, a passenger, had stated that he "saw land about one mile and a half ahead at the time the Captain was in his cabin with the doctor. One of the officers went into the cabin and came out immediately. In about ten minutes the Captain came out, took a glance around and went in again." Melville also stated that Saxby, the third officer, "reported land to the Captain and received answer not to bother him but to call him when the ship was on the beach". Another passenger, Lyndon B. Carpenter, stated: "About three quarters of an hour before the vessel struck, Miss Hart was taken into the Captain's cabin by the Doctor, lights were brought into the cabin and the Captain, Doctor and Miss Hart were seen by me in the cabin. I saw the Captain come out about half an hour before the vessel struck, look about him and go in again. I did not see him again until after the vessel struck but I heard him give some orders about five minutes before she struck. His conduct during the voyage had already weakened my confidence in him."

The Miss Hart referred to appears on the passenger list as an English spinster aged eighteen. One can only speculate whether involvement with her or feelings over parting from her were factors distracting Forbes from his duty. It is clear enough that his ship was not the matter of prime importance to him that night. James Hodges, the boatswain, stated that the captain did not appear for a quarter of an hour after all hands were piped. Then "he walked forward and spoke to me and I said it is almost time to put the helm down. He said there is plenty of time yet. We were not more at this time than half a mile from the land and we were not twenty yards from the reef which was on her lee. He put the helm down about ten minutes after he had said there was plenty of time." According to passenger Alexander Stockdall, "The master continued to scan the shore with his glass without issuing any order." Thomas Wilkinson, who was travelling with his wife and three children, said, "I was on the forecastle with Captain Forbes about quarter of an hour before the vessel struck and no order had been issued to go about. The anchor was not let go for fully an hour after she struck." Not one of the witnesses suggests that the captain was in any way unwell or appeared intoxicated.

There appeared to be an unanswerable case against Forbes, but despite this, the Chief Justice, the Honourable Sir William à Beckett, displayed reluctance from the outset to hear the case, probably because there was no precedent for it in the colony and no recognized guidelines. Nevertheless, Forbes appeared at the Melbourne Criminal Sessions of 21st February 1856.

A five-column report of the proceedings appeared in the *Argus*. For the first time really significant charges were laid, this time by the Solicitor-General: To preserve the *Schomberg* from destruction or serious damage, it was requisite for Forbes to alter course. "He wholly neglected and omitted to perform his said duty of altering the course of the said ship." It was requisite for him to "keep . . . a due and proper distance from . . . shore", a duty he "wholly neglected and omitted to perform" and this "caused the destruction of the said ship. Also, he wholly neglected to keep watch." And again the matter of the anchor was alluded to.

The Solicitor-General followed up the charges with what seemed an irrefutable case.

At about nine o'clock in the night in question something was discerned in the distance which the defendant pronounced to be land . . . it proved to be so. It would appear that after this he was very little on deck, but went down into the cabin where he remained some time with the doctor and a lady who was on board, apparently careless of the safety of the vessel.

The first negligence imputed to the defendant was the having brought the ship into that place at all; it was totally out of the proper course.

Then the matter of the anchor again:

It would appear that the passengers generally cried out, "Let go the anchors!" . . . one expostulated with the captain . . . when the latter answered, "No matter—the insurance is right", or something to that effect . . . .

The night was light, so that nothing prevented the captain from making his observations. He was near land and he knew it, so that he was bound to have taken every ordinary precaution. There were some causes which made peculiar caution necessary. It was the day after Christmas Day, a time of festivity at sea as well as on shore, and when a captain cannot always rely upon the sobriety of his men, and, as every seaman knows, very little reliance is to be placed upon the charts in use. The ship in question was very large and, especially by a captain who was not accustomed to coasting in Australia, ought not to have been run so close in shore.

Anyone knowing the beetling Otway coast must have recognized that the Solicitor-General was right. But he then went on to point out a difficulty: the persons most competent to give evidence "were the defendant's own officers, and it was difficult to find persons so situated towards the defendant to give evidence against him". Who indeed, loyalty apart, would stand against so formidable a master!

He [the Solicitor-General] did not know whether to attribute infatuation to the defendant, or that he merely wanted to prove his courage as a seaman. It might appear that his conduct savored somewhat of braggadocio, and that he was anxious to show his superior skill in going to the very verge of danger, and in then escaping it. It might be from a more laudable motive, namely, to shorten his passage, and so to advertise himself to future passengers. But it would be seen that under any circumstances he could not have gained a day.

To those who have read Fenwick's '*Lightning*' *Diary* and other references to Forbes's showy daring, the Solicitor-General's insight into the man seems extraordinarily near the mark. Witnesses were then called—but not one of them a *Schomberg* officer.

First was James Hodges, boatswain. He was under something of a cloud, as it had been alleged at Williamstown Court that passengers and, indeed, Mr Shillinglaw of the Water Police, had bribed him. But his statement was clear, and one gains a mounting impression of a man trying to tell "the whole truth", but foredoomed by his lack of familiarity with the legal stratagem of discrediting a witness.

Counsel for Captain Forbes, this time Messrs Dawson, Wright, and Fellows, dismembered Hodges. He was not entitled to give such evidence, they declared, unless he were legally qualified to navigate a ship. "It was like an unqualified person giving medical evidence." Undoubtedly they knew he was not qualified; undoubtedly they also knew that faulty seamanship not faulty navigation had caused the wreck. Navigation had ceased once Forbes began coasting.

Hodges protested that he had "passed an examination as boatswain in the Queen's service. I was about eight years in the Queen's service and have been twenty years at sea. I have sailed with Capt. Forbes better than four years. I was chief mate of the *Flora MacDonald** under Capt. Forbes."

But did Mr Hodges know how to use logarithms? Alas, he only knew that they were necessary for navigation. Then he blundered by telling the Chief Justice that "the upper part of the chart was east". (This probably explains his puzzling "we stood out to the westward" instead of southward). When laughter at this gaffe had subsided, he said simply, "I know I am not a navigator but I am a seaman." There was dogged pride and courage in the words. Undoubtedly he had competently assessed the danger, but had expected orders.

"The whole of the crew remained by the ship until night," he continued, "when the chief mate told them to go on shore. I remained by ‑the ship until that time. In point of fact, neither I nor any of the crew deserted ship." (This had been alleged in

---

* The *Flora MacDonald*, 674 tons, was another of Baines's ships. She sailed from Liverpool to Portland in 1852 when Captain Forbes was on the *Marco Polo*. Forbes does not appear to have brought her to Australia.

some of the newspapers.) "I never declined doing my duty. We returned to the ship, and remained until we were ordered ashore. Capt. Forbes remained in the ship all the time. He and the chief mate said they would stand by the ship while one plank adhered to another."

But Forbes's counsel soon had Hodges utterly confused. The court reporter records, "The witness here contradicted himself . . . he appeared not to understand the questions put to him." His last forlorn answer was, "I had received no wages from the owners, and was starving about the streets at the time the passengers paid me 8s. to pay my expenses." But by now he was effectively discredited. The discrediting had not been done by Forbes, but one would hope that he had pangs of conscience at the doing of it.

The next two witnesses were passengers. They were fumbling from the outset, nevertheless a telling sentence came from one: "I could hear the roar of breakers before the order was given to 'bout ship." A third passenger "appeared to know nothing about the case".

Even Captain Matthews, Lloyd's agent, who had been twenty years at sea, could give no evidence of worth, since he did not know the Otway coast. But Captain Doran, who had rescued the passengers, knew the coast well, as he plied regularly between Melbourne and Warrnambool. Cautiously he said, "Perhaps I might not have gone within four or five miles. . . . According to the evidence I have heard today, I would not have gone so near the shore if I could have avoided it. . . . It is impossible to give an opinion as to what should have been done, except with a full knowledge of all the circumstances." Who was he, a colonial coastal captain, to cast doubt on Britain's most famous clipper captain!

This ended the case for the Crown. Counsel for Captain Forbes submitted "that there was no case against the defendant. There was no evidence of Capt. Forbes having omitted to do any single act by which the ship might have been preserved from immediate destruction." The Chief Justice agreed "and directed the jury to find accordingly". Which of course they did.

As a *coup de grâce* Captain Forbes's counsel "wished to state on behalf of the defendant that nearly all his cabin passengers, all his officers, and about twenty merchant captains had come to the court to give evidence, some of fact and others of nautical skill, on behalf of the defendant, if the case for the prosecution had not failed".

The case ended on Friday 22nd February. The *Argus* of the following Monday carried a scathing editorial:

Never before in the history of these colonies has so much interest been excited by a wreck (not involving loss of life) as by that of the *Schomberg*, and so strong has been the feeling against Captain Forbes that nothing short of his being brought to trial would have satisfied the public mind. This trial was, in fact, even by the friends of Captain Forbes, deemed necessary, because it was by them looked upon as the only means by which his character could be cleared.

By some extraordinary hallucination the Chief Justice has been prevented from appreciating the nature and importance of the trial, and he has arbitrarily deprived the public of that thorough investigation and decision of a competent tribunal which for the sake of the highest interests of the community, were imperatively required. . . . The offence with which Captain Forbes was charged was one involving danger to the lives of hundreds of human beings, and loss of property to a very large amount, causing ruin to numbers of industrious men cast penniless on a strange country, fifteen thousand miles from their home and friends, discouraging the commercial interests of this colony. If true, he was a malefactor of the worst character, for his crime was one against society at large; and yet this it was in which the Chief Justice thought proper to apply the rule that would regulate him in the case of petty theft.

What, we ask the Chief Justice, is the reason why a court-martial is held when a ship-of-war is lost? It is not on account of the mere pecuniary loss to the nation; it is not simply for the sake of the individual officers in charge of the vessel; it is still more for the satisfaction of the nation, and as a terror to others. It was on the same principle that Captain Forbes was placed on his trial, and, by the course pursued, the Chief Justice has baulked the principal object which for the sake of the individual and the community was alike required.

Captain Forbes had in his charge several hundreds of intending colonists. He had one of the finest ships and largest cargoes ever brought to these shores. A great part of the cargo was machinery and plant for our railways, which cannot be replaced for nearly a year, and so far our progress in this respect is retarded. With all this valuable freight, it is alleged that he brought his ship close to a shore to him unknown, and that through his deliberate negligence the vessel and cargo were destroyed. It was the truth or falsity of this charge that the public desired to know.

What is the result? Are the people satisfied? Is the reputation of Captain Forbes vindicated? And, above all, what security does the trial afford that the offences charged against Captain Forbes may not with impunity be perpetrated?

We much regret that we cannot conscientiously give a satisfactory answer to any one of these queries.

14
DECLINE

Captain Forbes left Melbourne very soon after his acquittal; he reached Liverpool before mid-May. A letter appeared from him there in the *Daily News*:

SIR,

I learned on my arrival here, on Saturday night, by the *Ocean Chief*, that a report of an "indignation meeting" held in Melbourne, 3rd January past, by some of the passengers who went out in the ill-fated ship *Schomberg*, appeared in your columns. As that report was entirely one-sided, and did me a grievous wrong, I am sure you will have no objection to insert the report of my trial and acquittal in the Supreme Court of Victoria.

You will see that the Court and jury did not require to hear my defence; and you will see, by the letters I enclose, that all the cabin passengers but one expressed their sympathy for me, and were pleased to testify to my conduct during the passage. There were two charges against me—one for immoral conduct, and one for bad seamanship. There was also a charge against the ship of supplying bad provisions. The first charge against myself, and the charge against the vessel, were dismissed instantly by the Court; and in the report of the trial you will see that my character as a sailor remains unaffected.

My moral character is still more dear to me than even my professional character; and, unfortunately for me, my accusers coupled with me in iniquity the surgeon of the ship. That gentleman, you will see by a report in the "Fifeshire Advertiser" of Saturday last, has been tried in an ecclesiastical court, and, as might be expected from his character and years, has been fully exonerated from the infamous accusation.

. . . I confess to a large amount of mental affliction at the sad interruption to a voyage that so far I took pride in; but perhaps you will not refuse the consolation afforded me by reminding you that I was the first captain of a vessel that made a rapid passage from Australia to England, having on that occasion sailed round the world in four months and thirteen days.

The same paper carried a paragraph from the Glasgow *Herald*:

At a meeting of the session of the parish church, Kirkaldy, on Wednesday, Dr. Hardy, as a member of that body, emitted voluntarily a declaration in relation to the rumours affecting his moral and Christian character while acting as surgeon in the ship *Schomberg*. The decision of the session was, that they were unanimously of opinion that Dr. Hardy had fully vindicated himself from all allegations brought against him, which they had no hesitation in pronouncing false and calumnious.

Hardy scarcely matters. What of his famous master? It is unlikely that evidence will come to light so long after the wreck which might explain Forbes's lack of action. The contents of the letters expressing sympathy for him will likewise never be known. With his officers and cabin passengers supporting him, is the whole thing to be regarded as malicious fabrication by those of lower station? Hardly. Indisputably the *Schomberg* ought to have been much farther out to sea. It is scarcely to be believed that Forbes lacked the skill to take her farther out. Was he then wittingly running a great risk to be an exhibitionist, as he had often done before? Or was he giving the ship scant attention? Distasteful though the tone of the protest meeting had been, one can scarcely escape the conclusion that Forbes had female distractions—it would be surprising if so famous and colourful a man had not been attractive to women. Also there is the coincidence of Christmas festivities with the landfall. The most familiar accusation against Forbes, repeated by Joseph W. Foley in *Three Liverpool Worthies*, is that when the mate informed him they were close to land, "Forbes, who was playing cards, took no notice and stayed to finish the rubber." When he came on deck, "report has it that [he] said in disgust, 'Let her go to hell, and tell me when she is high and dry.'" Although reports of his words must be regarded as suspect, one can scarcely escape a conclusion of negligence.

It has frequently been stated that Forbes was never given another command by Baines, but this is not so. Although he remained ashore for a time, he was appointed by Baines to the *Hastings* in 1857 and took her to Moreton Bay on 12th February that year. This might have been a gesture of friendship by Baines, an attempt to help Forbes rehabilitate himself. If so, the gesture was largely wasted. Although Forbes became sole owner of the *Hastings* before the end of the year, she was in poor shape and put back to Sydney in a sinking condition after having set out from Moreton Bay for Bombay.

For Forbes, things were going from bad to worse. The *Moreton Bay Paper* of 18th July 1857 reported a charge against him of having forcibly pressed his advances on a woman in Brisbane. "Captain Forbes, formerly of the royal mail-ship *Schomberg*, and now of the *Hastings*, appeared at the Police Office, in discharge of bail, to defend himself against an accusation preferred by a servant of Mr. G. S. Warry of this town, of having assaulted her on the evening of the third day's races." Unfortunately for Forbes's waning reputation, the charge was evidently exaggerated. the assault being "with intent to commit a rape". "Having carefully noted down the evidence," the paper continued, "we have no hesitation in saying that there were very slight grounds indeed for preferring a grave charge of this kind against the defendant, and we are justified in expressing this opinion by the facts elicited in the course of cross examination of the witnesses, and particularly that of the prosecutrix herself. Had the defendant been charged with a common assault, it is very likely he would have been convicted and fined, perhaps the heaviest penalty for such an offence; for it is absolutely necessary, for the sake of public morality and public decency, that virtuous females should be protected against the libertine advances of amorous gentlemen like Captain Forbes, who, it appears, has this time 'caught a tartar'." The case was dismissed.

By a piece of contrasting irony, it was at this time, in Melbourne, that John F. Millar was nominated for the gold medal of the Shipwrecked Fishermen's and Mariners' Royal Benevolent Society for his bravery on the night of the wreck of the *Schomberg*. He was the passenger who "volunteered to take charge of the boat to look for a landing place; and when he was coming back to the ship, unsuccessful, he saved the lives of a boatful of passengers by preventing their attempt to land on an unknown shore". How it was that he was unsuccessful is unaccountable; the open beaches of what is known now as Newfield Bay were only a few hundred yards off.

If Forbes was breaking up, so was the *Hastings*. By 1859 she belonged to Johnson & Co. of Liverpool and was being used in the lowly guano trade. Late that year she sailed from the Kuira Muria Islands in the Arabian Sea, again under Captain Forbes, with guano for Liverpool. On 28th December, about a hundred and thirty miles up the coast from Port Elizabeth, she was found by the French bark *Chevreuil* "in a sinking state . . . having seven feet of water in the hold". This report from the *Cape Mercantile Advertiser* went on to relate that the *Hastings* "was, at that time, settling fast by the head". The master of the *Chevreuil* took off Captain Forbes and his crew.

The *Hastings* remained afloat a little longer; she was boarded next day, 29th December, by men from the *Craigevar*. Finding that the chronometers and ship's papers had gone, they realized that the crew must have been picked up; nevertheless, they attempted to tow her. Next day, "in consequence of a heavy gale . . . off Cape Padrone" they were compelled to abandon her.

The gale finished her. The *Eastern Province Herald* of 10th January published reports from Grahamstown "that portions of a wreck have been washed up to the Westward of the Kowie. They consist of spars, boats, seamen's chests, and a quantity of loose timber. . . . The whole beach, as far as the Three Sisters, is strewed with pieces of timber. There can scarcely be a doubt that these belong to the *Hastings*."

In Cape Town Captain Forbes offered "to reimburse the French captain [of the *Chevreuil*] for the losses caused by delay etc.; but that officer has liberally refused to accept any remuneration whatever for his services".

The *Hastings* was lost four years almost to the day after the *Schomberg*. It must have been a saddened, subdued "Bully"

Forbes who left for Liverpool by the steamer *Celt* on 20th January 1860. Although aged only thirty-nine, Forbes's brief time at the pinnacle of his profession had fallen behind; gone too was the Golden Decade in Victoria that had given him his opportunity.

Lubbock records that in 1862 he was "home again and acting as agent for the owners of the Glasgow ship *Earl of Derby*, which was in distress on the Donegal Coast". Baines had not forgotten him, but Baines had amalgamated with Gibbs, Bright & Co. Probably through his influence, Forbes was given command in 1863 of the *General Wyndham*—this at the time of the cotton famine. He sailed for Calcutta on 13th June, then on to China on 19th December. Lubbock describes him at this time as "a seedy, broken-down looking skipper, with the forced joviality of a broken-hearted man. He discussed the passage down the China Seas (it was S.W. monsoon time) with some of the tea clipper captains, and displayed all his old bravado, declaring he would 'force a passage.' However in spite of his big talk, he took 50 days to Anjer.

"I have come across one characteristic story of his visit to Hongkong," Lubbock continues. "He was insulted by two Americans on the Water Front; in a moment he had his coat off and did not let up until he had given them a good thrashing."

In that same year, 1864, Jane Forbes died, aged only thirty-three. She was buried in Smithdown Road Cemetery, Liverpool. Who cared then for the Forbes's daughters is not known. "Bully" himself returned to the *General Wyndham* in September 1865 and sailed for Charleston, U.S.A. He was discharged from her on return to Liverpool on 5th February 1866. Then, in a sad farewell to the sea, he returned in 1867 to his first love, the *Marco Polo*. She had suffered collision with an iceberg and, like Forbes, was much past her best. For all that it seems appropriate that his last voyage should have been in her. He sailed from Liverpool on 30th January for Mobile, presumably for cotton, and was discharged back in Liverpool on 19th August the same year. He retired to 78 Westbourne Street, Liverpool, aged only forty-six.

Although Baines was eventually to survive Forbes by seventeen years, his financial decline had begun with his amalgamation in auxiliary steam with Gibbs, Bright; the failure of Barnard's Bank finished him. To quote again from Lubbock:

. . . for some years before his death, [Baines] had to depend for his subsistence on the charity of his friends. Indeed he was absolutely penniless when he died of dropsy on 8th March, 1889, in a common Liverpool lodging house. . . . Yet it will be a very long time before he and his celebrated ships are forgotten in Liverpool:

> In the Black Ball Line I served my time,
> Hurrah! for the Black Ball Line.

Forbes died at home from pneumonia on 13th June 1874. The Liverpool *Mercury* devoted a third editorial to him:

The Australian "gold fever", as it was called, will still be in the recollection of the commercial community of Liverpool. When Sir R. Murchison's prediction of the abundant existence of the precious metal at the antipodes was realised, there was a great rush of emigrants to that part of the world. To get to the New Eldorado as quickly as possible was the aim of thousands. Fast clipper ships came into sudden and great demand, and pushing, daring captains who could make a smart voyage found ready employment at every principal port of the kingdom. While the "fever" was at its height, a navigator of the character then wanted made his appearance in Liverpool, and, by the extraordinary rapidity of the voyages of his ship, and the luck that attended him in bringing large consignments of gold and wool to this country, was in no small degree instrumental in making Liverpool the chief port of emigration and the exportation of produce. This officer who died yesterday was Captain James Nicol Forbes.

The *Mercury* then sketched his early years, as quoted in chapter 6. It continued:

His unrivalled passages in [the *Marco Polo*] established the fame of the Black Ball Line throughout the country, and in a short time Liverpool had almost a monopoly of the Australian emigration trade. The success of Captain Forbes is easily explained. He was the first mercantile captain who carried out Maury's system of great-circle sailing, which is now so generally adopted. He was also a great believer in the utility of ships built upon what is called the thorough clipper line, and those sent from the yards of the Halls of Aberdeen and Donald McKay of Boston—such as the *Marco Polo*, the *Lightning*, the *Schomberg*, and The *Donald McKay*—were held by him to be models of marine architecture. There are no class of men more liable to vicissitude than those who follow the sea, and Captain Forbes had his disappointments as well as his successes. The loss of the *Schomberg* was a turning point in his career. But he met his subsequent misfortunes bravely. "Aberdeen" Forbes as he was familiarly called, will long be remembered as the founder of what may be termed a new school of navigation.

Soon after this editorial had appeared, John T. Towson, the great student of navigation, wrote to the *Mercury*. An extract of his letter is quoted for its praise of Forbes. The comparison of Maury's and Towson's directions to mariners is obscure for anyone but a historian of navigation.

GENTLEMEN,

I have read with much interest your article on "The late Captain Forbes". The whole of your remarks bearing testimony to his worth as a practical navigator I fully endorse. His unrivalled passages established the fame of Liverpool ships. . . . But I must, in self-defence, object to your remarks that follow. You say that "he was the first mercantile captain who carried out Maury's system of great-circle sailing, which is now so generally adopted." I have now before me a letter from Maury, in which he disavows any services rendered by himself in connection with either great-circle, composite, or windward-great-circle sailing, but gives me the fullest credit for these. I have also a paper written by the late Captain Forbes—in connection with a testimonial presented to me in 1857, of over £1000, by the merchants, principally of Liverpool —stating that he had succeeded by carrying out my theory. Far be it from me to undervalue in any way the services rendered by the late Captain Forbes. Without the aid of such practical seamen as Godfrey, Boyce, but most especially Forbes, my labours would have resulted in mere dry theories on paper. These practical men have given them a vitality and value. But, still, the service I have rendered I cannot allow, in silence, to be awarded to another.

For his unbroken sailing-ship records alone, Forbes is worthy of a niche in Australian history. His very success probably sped his downfall. A superb and fearless mariner, he did not hold to the balancing virtues of patience and prudence. If he let the *Schomberg* "go to hell", like a woman who had spurned him, she in turn put him through hell for neglect of her. At the end he was buried beside his wife. His grave bears the proud words, THE LATE COMMANDER OF THE CELEBRATED CLIPPER SHIP MARCO POLO.

It would have pleased him to know that a replica of the *Marco Polo* is being built at St. John, New Brunswick, in the same yard as the original, the ship he so loved.

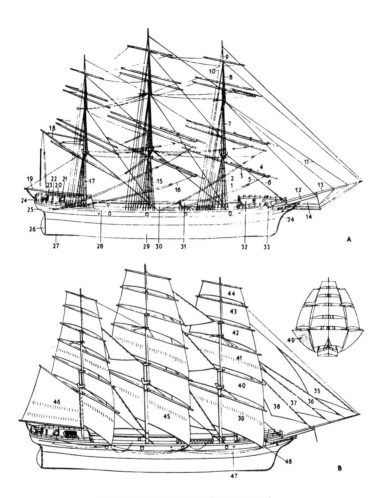

SHIP: A. RIGGING. B. SAILS (SQUARE-RIGGED)

A. Masts, spars, and rigging: 1. Foremast. 2. Fore shrouds. 3. Fore-lower yard. 4. Stunsail boom. 5. Fore brace. 6. Forestay. 7. Fore topmast. 8. Fore-topgallant mast. 9. Fore-royal mast. 10. Fore-royal backstay. 11. Jib-stays. 12. Bowsprit. 13. Jib-boom. 14. Bobstay. 15. Main-mast. 16. Mainbrace. 17. Mizzen-mast. 18. Gaff. 19. Boom. Decks and hull: 20. Poop. 21. Companionway. 22. Binnacle (holding compass). 23. Wheel or helm. 24. Taffrail. 25. Counter. 26. Rudder. 27. Keel. 28. Bulwarks. 29. Bilge. 30. Waist or amidships. 31. Deck-house (with galley). 32. Forecastle. 33. Cat-head. 34. Stem. B. Sails: 35. Flying jib. 36. Outer jib. 37. Inner jib. 38. Fore-topmast staysail. 39. Foresail or fore-course. 40. Fore-lower topsail. 41. Fore-upper topsail. 42. Fore-lower topgallant sail. 43. Fore-upper topgallant sail. 44. Fore-royal. 45. Mainsail. 46. Spanker. 47. Fore-tack. 48. Fore-sheet. 49. Fore-lower stunsail.
(The names of the upper masts, sails, yards, stays, and braces attached to the main- and mizzen-masts follow those given for the foremast)

THE WRECK
of the
LOCH ARD:
END OF A SHIP,
END OF AN ERA

15
A WARNING BEACON

Although "Bully" Forbes's career was a meteoric one, the wreck that brought his downfall was not attended by loss of life; the circumstances of the wreck of the *Schomberg* were not even particularly dramatic. This was far from the case with the tragic wreck of the *Loch Ard*. The *Illustrated Sydney News* was to remark that, "since the wreck of the *Dunbar* off South Head [Sydney] in 1857, no marine disaster in Australian waters has been so alarming or caused so much sensation as the loss of the *Loch Ard*". Added to this was the fact that the only two survivors were a boy and a girl, both aged eighteen. They lent the wreck an aura of romance it has never lost and brought it a place in Australian folk history.

But the wreck has significance for less obvious reasons: it coincided with the end of the long era of passenger-carrying to Australia by sail; the *Loch Ard* was, in fact, the last sailing ship to lose lives of passengers through failure to negotiate the western entrance of Bass Strait.

The two sides of the western entrance may be imagined as a trap awaiting mariners, its more dangerous jaw undoubtedly being the southern or Cape Wickham one. During the twenty-three years that passed between the wreck of the *Schomberg* and the wreck of the *Loch Ard*, a lighthouse had been erected there. This was done in 1861. There had been a good deal of lobbying against such a light by some masters and owners who contended that in conditions of poor visibility it might well be mistaken for Otway. Masters making this error would naturally alter course to starboard, thinking to skirt Otway, and so would be led onto King Island's western coast—the greatest graveyard of ships in Australia.

In 1859, when erection of the lighthouse at Cape Wickham was recommended, even the recommendation was made with reservation. *Admiralty Sailing Directions* for Australia read:

In advising the erection of a lighthouse in the neighbourhood of Cape Wickham, the Commissioners wish to guard themselves from affording the public any reasonable supposition that this light can be at all considered in a position of a great highway light for the navigation of Bass Strait. The light at Cape Wickham can only be regarded as a beacon warning navigators of danger, rather than a leading light to a great thoroughfare.

Because the coast was relatively low and the lighthouse had to withstand violent weather, Wickham was constructed on massive lines. Its foundations went thirty feet into the earth; it was built of granite with walls eleven feet thick at the base; it was 145 feet high, the light itself being 280 feet above the sea. Surprisingly, a signal station was established adjacent to the new light. To exchange visual signals ships often needed to approach dangerously close to the station, a risk not officially admitted for fifty years.

On 1st November 1861 the lamp was lighted—a bright, fixed light. At Otway on clear nights Ford could see it "as a star with bright loom". Distant though it was, it was at least an indication to him that guardianship of the western entrance was at last shared.

The Wickham journal has survived and in it one may read the head keeper's frequent references to violent weather:

December 15th 1861: Rain very heavy. No moderation of gale. Superintendent up all night . . .
July 21st 1862: 5 p.m. Just as the assistants were about to go to the light-house a furious squall detained them. A fireball burst striking the tower and proceeded to earth by inner bell wire, scathing all vegetation in its passage. Made a heavy report as of a shotted gun . . .
July 4th 1863: Dark gloomy weather . . . Noon. Blowing a tremendous gale, rooting up much vegetation and damaging roofs of cottages. Sunset. Gale at its maximum, being almost a hurricane . . . Lantern

vibrating fearfully and the noise of the wind one continued roar. Could not perceive any sign of weakness through the immense pressure on it.

The superintendent, or head keeper, Mr E. C. Spong, came to the position in 1862. He succeeded Captain F. Drugan who resigned in his first year after "much abuse and bad language from William McKean. . . . His abuse and treacherous talk compels me to avoid the light room during the time he is there." Spong must have been cast more in the mould of Ford, for he was to remain at Wickham for twenty years.

Even though the Wickham light was steady and the Otway light flashing, there is evidence that on at least one occasion the two were confused. In July 1865 the Wickham keeper reported "loss of the British three-masted schooner *Arrow* in the very heavy gale of 24th and 25th . . . Light was seen but mistaken for Otway."

In the next year the *Netherby*, a Black Ball ship, was driven before storms for a fortnight so that everything on her decks was smashed. She was carrying 452 emigrants and a crew of fifty from London to Brisbane. Unable to determine where she was, she struck the west coast of King Island soon after 7 p.m. on 14th July. Most of the boats were swamped as soon as they were launched, but by some means left unrecorded a line was got ashore and made fast there. The one remaining boat was pulled back and forth along this line, and everyone was safely landed.

Although this large group of survivors was able to obtain food supplies from the ship and from the abundant local game, the captain did not know where he was. Four days after the wreck the Wickham keeper recorded: "10 a.m. the Second Officer and six passengers arrived at the station from the wreck of the *Netherby* and reported that she was stranded at 7 p.m. July 14th with 451 souls on board, all saved. They had been 4 days coming up and were very nearly exhausted."

After having led this party to the lighthouse, Second Officer Parry crossed Bass Strait in the station whaleboat and landed at a point near Torquay. At a sheep-station there he broke the news which was then taken to Geelong and telegraphed through to Melbourne. In the meantime Spong had quartered large numbers of the survivors at the lighthouse settlement. All were finally taken to Melbourne in two Victorian government steamers and were cared for at the Exhibition Building.

Nine years later a greater disaster was to occur at King Island. The storm on this occasion caught three well-known ships in Bass Strait. One was lost; two narrowly survived, one of the two being the Loch Line ship *Loch Ard*, then on her maiden voyage.

16
THE LOCH LINE

The softwood hulls of the gold clippers had served their decade well, but they had not been built for prolonged life, nor were their slim lines designed for commodious cargo space. Their function had been to take would-be miners as quickly as possible from one end of the earth to the other.

For the shipping companies the gold bonanza was over. A new type of immigrant was being attracted to Australia, the family man who intended to remain, a more sober individual with better business sense. He expected improved conditions on the voyage out for his wife and family. For their part the companies recognized that if they were going to attract such passengers in the face of increasing competition from steamships, they would have to emphasize comfort rather than speed—journeys free of smoke and engine noise, yet just as fast as steam.

Even before the gold decade had begun, a screw steamer built of iron and carrying sail—Isambard Kingdom Brunel's *Great Britain*—had proved herself on the Atlantic, making her first voyage from Liverpool to New York in 1845. A giant of 4000 tons, 322 feet long, with six masts and powered by four direct action cylinders, she later ran aground off Ireland. Purchased by Gibbs, Bright for the Australian run, she was refloated and repaired. It was as well for sailing ships that she initially had coaling difficulties on the long journey; even so, she covered the distance to Melbourne in eighty-one days. This was as early as 1852. The sailing masters must have been relieved to see her taken off the run to become a troop transport, first to the Crimea, then to Calcutta. But in 1866 she returned and set a new record to Melbourne of fifty-nine days. In all she was to carry 9500 passengers to Australia in a period of ten years. Fortunately for sail, there was only one *Great Britain*; the rest they could still compete with.

In the 1860s some of the sailing ship companies began building of iron—iron hulls and, in many cases, masts of iron for half their height, and rigging of galvanized wire. The iron clippers were not generally as fine-lined as the gold clippers; their chief role was to carry miscellaneous cargoes out and wool home.

As iron lacked the resilience of wood, the new ships did not normally venture into the fifties, but confined themselves to the roaring forties. They were not as fast as the best of the gold clippers, but their owners left no doubt in their masters' minds that quick passages were expected of them; indeed, the strength of iron masts and wire rigging led designers to over-rig them in an attempt to gain more speed. As a result, dismastings were numerous.

One of the foremost authorities on the Loch ships in later years was George R. Leggett, himself a man of seafaring family (his father had taken the first settlers to King Island in 1859). Writing in the *Port of Melbourne Quarterly* as late as 1953, Leggett felt moved to place on record "the glorious work done by men and ships in carrying the Red Ensign to the uttermost parts of the world". In that year few indeed of the Loch masters were still alive.

In the story of the latter 19th century and early 20th century trade of the port of Melbourne, the famous Loch liners hold an almost legendary position. For more than half a century, dating from 1867, it was not possible to visit the waterfront in the Port of Melbourne without seeing one or more of those beautiful sailing ships, with their painted ports, either at anchor in Hobson's Bay or berthed at the wharves, loading or discharging cargoes. During the wool season up to seven of the liners might be seen in the port simultaneously. Their commanders, officers and apprentices were welcome visitors in the business houses and private homes and, in reality, the Loch Line became an integral part in building the prosperity of our State.

One gains an impression of impeccable masters. It was by no means always so. At a Marine Board inquiry held on 22nd January 1877 Captain John Meiklejohn, master of the *Loch Lomond*, was charged with "alleged drunkenness on board during the voyage". "Summary of Inquiry—Charge made by several first-class passengers of the almost constant state of drunkenness of the captain during the passage to Melbourne. . . . Result—The Board found the charge fully sustained, and suspended Captain Meiklejohn's certificate for eighteen months."

Captain William Branscombe, master of the *Loch Leven*, was less fortunate. Having left Melbourne in October 1871, he lost his ship when west-bound through Bass Strait. This was attributed to "the neglect of the master for not taking ordinary precautions of navigation". The Board was unable to deal with Captain Branscombe's certificate "in consequence of the unfortunate accident which deprived him of his life".

Having struck the northern tip of King Island, Branscombe tried to return to his ship by launching the same whaleboat that Parry of the *Netherby* had used to cross from Wickham to Torquay. His intention was to save the ship's papers, but the boat was overwhelmed by the seas and he was drowned. No other lives were lost.

Basil Lubbock has recorded that the Loch Line of Glasgow was founded in 1867 by William Aitken and James Lilburn, who had both gained considerable experience as shipping clerks in other well-known firms. Lilburn himself was an able yachtsman.

The ships carried first, second and third class passengers outwards, and when steam began to cut in they still held on until they were the last of all the sailing ships to continue carrying passengers. Many an invalid or consumptive has gained fresh vigor and untold benefit from a voyage to the Antipodes in a Loch liner. . . . The saloon fares charged were £40 to Adelaide and Melbourne, £42 to Sydney, £76 for the round trip out and home.

In trying to prove the superiority of sail, many Loch masters lost their ships and, ironically, proved the reverse. By sail the continents of the world had been discovered; it was hard indeed for its most skilled practitioners to recognize that its day was almost done.

When one reads of the long succession of disasters that befell the Loch ships (Appendix 3) one is tempted to agree with Leggett that there must have been a hoodoo on them. They were ill-fated to a degree extraordinary even in that era of uncertain sea travel. One of the most unfortunate of the line was the *Loch Ard.*

17
LOCH ARD

The *Loch Ard* was built in the Clyde by Barklay, Curle and Company in 1873; her official logbook was No. 68061. Of 1693 tons gross weight—compared with the *Schomberg*'s 2600—she was 262 feet 7 inches long, 38 feet wide and 23 feet deep. Her masts were almost 150 feet high—60 feet lower than those of the *Schomberg*. For all that, it was later suggested that she perhaps carried too much sail to be safely managed, even by the extremely capable men who sailed her.

She was launched on 8th November 1873. Evidently it was intended to rush her into departure for Melbourne. "In order to get the vessel away," states Leggett, "she was rigged in a hurry in bitterly cold weather. This caused the rigging to stretch and sag when the vessel began to pound into a hard westerly gale in the North Atlantic, with the result that she was dismasted."

She had sailed on 4th December under Captain F. J. Green. The dismasting occurred off the north-west coast of Ireland. Under jury rig she took three weeks to limp back to the Clyde, where she was unloaded and refitted. "While lying at Princess Pier, Greenock, a gale sprang up and the vessel was blown from the pier and grounded on a bank seven miles away, but she was undamaged, and at last got away for Melbourne."

This was on 6th January 1874. Whether any blame was attached to Captain Green is not known, but certainly the ship sailed under a new master, Captain W. Robertson. Departing for Melbourne in her company were the clippers *John Kerr* and *British Admiral*.

Captain Robertson's experience was to be a great deal worse than Captain Green's. In the southern Indian Ocean, over two hundred miles north-west of Kerguelen Island, the *Loch Ard* was struck by a gale so violent that "the topmast came down, bringing the foremast with it. The latter broke off at the deck and the whole of the wreck fell across the ship. The foremast in coming down carried away the main-stays, and the main-mast followed almost immediately and brought down the mizzen topmast." For four days she was almost helpless in mountainous seas. She was sighted by the *City of Berlin*, Captain Warden, and offered assistance. By then Captain Robertson believed they could extricate themselves without help. Under jury rig they began limping towards Australia. It says much for the men who sailed her that seven weeks later she reached Bass Strait. So did the *British Admiral* and the *John Kerr*, the latter also under jury rig.

Leggett describes the end of the voyage for the three of them: "Then one of the heaviest gales overtook the vessels, and the *Loch Ard* brought up with two anchors holding her off a lee shore at the back of Sorrento. The *John Kerr* was able to keep to sea and was at last towed in by the tugboat *Williams*. The other vessel, the *British Admiral*, went ashore on King Island in the same gale with the loss of all except nine men."

The wreck of the *British Admiral* occurred at 2.30 a.m. on a reef about a mile from shore. A tablet at Admiral Bay, as it subsequently became known, reads: "To the Memory of William Dalzell Nicholson, Third son of the Hon. Wm. Nicholson, who, along with 78 others, perished in the wreck of the *British Admiral*, 23rd May 1874, aged 25 years. 'To live in the hearts we leave behind is not to die.'"

An artist's sketch of the *Loch Ard* at the end of this first voyage shows her limping past Point Nepean, shorn of her canvas splendour, with only iron stumps of masts standing. Repaired in Melbourne, she returned to London, then made a further voyage out under Captain Robertson.

Upon returning from this voyage Captain Robertson transferred to the *Loch Vennachar*, and while holding this command he died. His successor on the *Loch Ard* also died on the ship's next voyage. This was Captain C. Buchanan, who took the *Loch Ard* to Calcutta, where she again came close to disaster, on this occasion through running aground in the Hooghly. Presumably she was taken back to Glasgow by her first officer. Command of her on her fourth voyage passed to Captain J. Mackay, who made only the one voyage in her, departing from Glasgow for Melbourne on 7th February 1877 and arriving in London on New Year's Day 1878. It was at this stage, when the *Loch Ard* was five years old, that command of her passed to Captain George Gibb.

18
CAPTAIN AND
COMPLEMENT

Little can be learnt of George Gibb's background except that he was born at Kincardine, Perthshire, in 1849, the third of four sons, all of whom became master mariners; that he gained master's certificate No. 87273, and that he married Miss Annie McMeekan, aged 20, on January 14th 1878, some six weeks before he departed from London for Melbourne as master of the *Loch Ard*. He was then aged 28. Some newspapers of the day had it that the *Loch Ard* voyage was his first to Australia, but this seems most improbable. Whatever the truth, he was to prove himself an able and conscientious master, courageous and most considerate of his passengers.

Gibb's crew numbered thirty-six—thirty-seven if one includes the ship's doctor. This doctor was a Dublin man, Evory Carmichael. Dr. Carmichael "was a man of means and only obliged to come to Australia on account of his health." Aged forty-five, he suffered from tubercolosis and was emigrating to Queensland with his family; they had relatives near Maryborough. He was offered the post on the *Loch Ard* for the nominal sum of a shilling a month with free accommodation in the first-class quarters.

The names of the other members of the crew as they appear on the ship's papers were: Thomas McLauchlan (first mate), George K. Baxter (second mate), Ernest A. Atkinson, (third mate), James Runcie (carpenter), R. Hunt (boatswain), Robert Fox (sailmaker),

George Clay Inch (steward), Rowland Giles (cook), Thomas Heselton, G. McNeil, John McGemily, E. Videl, N.M. Grangvist, John Johnson, John Egan, Charles Cameron, George Freeman, Joseph King, William Legg, William Wright, George Skinner, John Brooks, Thomas King, George Smith, James Wood, Henry Anderson, C. Archer, Magnus Murray (all able seamen), F.T. Fincham (ordinary seaman), Henry Donohue (engine driver), William Johnson (lamp trimmer or cook's mate), Charles Spicer (second steward); Robert Strasenbergh, Thomas Pearce, W.H. Stevenson (apprentices).

In this crew the apprentice Tom Pearce had an uncle and a cousin, but who among the thirty-six they were is not known—possibly the two Johnsons. It is known, however, that Pearce and Robert Strasenbergh were particularly close friends.

Nearly half the passenger list consisted of members of the Carmichael family. The others listed were Mr. and Mrs. John Stuckey, a young couple with relatives already in Australia, Reginald Jones, George Yates, Thomas Pitt, H.R. Godley, C. Collingwood and Gerrard Rolleston. All of these were travelling first class. In the second class accommodation were Arthur Mitchell and the two Carmichael boys, Evory and Thomas. The Carmichael girls, Rebecca (Raby) aged twenty, and Eva, eighteen, and their two small sisters Margaret (Meta) and Annie, were all travelling first class. Their mother, a woman of forty, was also Rebecca Carmichael (nee Vige).

The one member of the Carmichael family not travelling on the *Loch Ard* was William, the eldest son. Some time earlier he had quarrelled with his father and had run away to sea. He was destined to live a wandering, restless life, but he appears to have been for a time much attracted to Australia and wrote urging his father to emigrate. Since their exchange of letters took six months or more, William was unaware that his father had decided to come. Rather impulsively he returned to Ireland with a view to persuading the family to follow his advice. Somewhere at sea his ship must have passed the *Loch Ard* and when he arrived in Dublin it was to find the family gone.

In all, the *Loch Ard* carried fifty-three souls. Mr. and Mrs. Stuckey were quartered close to Dr. and Mrs. Carmichael.

presumably in saloon accommodation. The young Carmichael girls, Meta and Annie, appear to have shared with their parents, while the older girls, Raby and Eva, were close by. The two Carmichael boys were evidently in another part of the ship, probably in the forward section of the 'tween-decks area.

Three members of a Mackay family had also booked on the ship, but "missed their passage".

Accommodation on the *Loch Ard* was very good indeed. In the stern, under the raised poop deck, was the first-class saloon accommodation. Directly over the heads of these passengers were the helm and binnacle, where the officers of the watch were stationed. This was the command centre of the ship; there the daily sextant observations were taken and compass directions given the helmsman.

Most of the passenger accommodation was in the 'tween-decks. All these sections—the poop, the upper deck, the deckhouse, containing the galley—were of wood; below, all was iron.

Most of the crew were accommodated with a good deal less comfort in the forecastle. Hemmed there between the converging iron walls of the bows, they had for company the reverberating impact of waves.

The *Loch Ard* carried a miscellaneous cargo, much of it consisting of homely articles not yet manufactured in quantity in the Colony: straw hats, umbrellas, perfumery, clay pipes, pianos, clocks, confectionery, linen, candles. By far the heavier part of the cargo consisted of railway lines, cement, iron, lead, and copper (see Appendix 5). Later it was suggested that the rails and the iron might have affected the ship's compasses to a degree not anticipated, but it is certain that the compasses had been "swung" at Gravesend before the ship departed and their deviation checked on all headings.

Incongruous in such a cargo was the most valuable single item carried: a porcelain peacock five feet high, made by Mintons of England in 1851. It had been packed with great care in a case and consigned in the captain's keeping. It was planned to exhibit it in the Sydney exhibition of 1879 and the Melbourne exhibition of 1880. In all, five such peacocks had been modelled for Mintons by Paul Comolera, a celebrated artist and sculptor of Limoges.

Another single item of considerable value was a Cremona violin consigned in a brass case to a Mr Palmer of Hamilton, Victoria.

All told, the cargo was valued at £53,000 and was insured with various Australian and New Zealand companies for £30,000.

Both the *Schomberg* and the *Loch Ard* were lost as their masters prepared to round Cape Otway. In the Gold Rush days this cape was sometimes the first land sighted after leaving the British Isles. (Photograph by courtesy of Ken Stepnell.)

Henry Bayles Ford, a former sea captain, was appointed as head keeper to the Cape Otway lighthouse in 1848. He remained thirty years until soon after the wreck of the *Loch Ard* in 1878. His son George played a notable part in the aftermath of the wreck. (Photograph by courtesy of Mrs V.F. Letcher)

In this ship, the *Marco Polo*, Captain James Nicol Forbes established his reputation. In 1852 he brought over 900 immigrants from Liverpool to Melbourne in 68 days, halving the usual passage time. (By courtesy of the State Library of Victoria.)

Captain Forbes' signature on the manifest for the *Marco Polo*'s second voyage to Melbourne 1853. (By courtesy of the State Library of Victoria.)

3.

Melbourne an feeling

SUMMARY.

	NUMBER OF SOULS.					EQUAL TO STATUTE ADULTS.
	ENGLISH.	SCOTCH.	IRISH.	OTHER COUNTRIES.	TOTAL.	
ADULTS	157	15	18	—	240	240
CHILDREN BETWEEN 12 AND 1	32	4	3		39	19½
INFANTS	8	1			9	
TOTAL	197	20	21		288	259½

We hereby certify, That the above is a correct List of the Names and Descriptions of all the Passengers who embarked at the Port of Liverpool.

Signed _James Nicol Forbes_ Master.

M. Smithson JPM Emigration Officer.

Countersigned _____ Officer of Customs at Liverpool.

4.

The *Lightning* depicted in full sail by Jack Spurling. In her Captain Forbes set a Melbourne-Liverpool record for sail that has never been eclipsed—just under 63 days. (By courtesy of Calendars of Distinction).

5.

The magnificent 2600 ton *Schomberg* which Captain Forbes ran onto a reef off Peterborough, Victoria. It cost him his reputation. (By courtesy of the National Maritime Museum, Greenwich.)

7.

Captain George Gibb. When he commanded the *Loch Ard* on her fatal voyage Captain Gibb was aged twenty-nine and not long married. (By courtesy of the State Library of Victoria.)

8.

Eva Carmichael (right) with her mother (centre) and her elder sister Rebecca (Raby) photographed shortly before they left Ireland. The bodies of Mrs. Carmichael and Raby were washed into the gorge; they were buried in the cliff-top cemetery. (By courtesy of Robert Townsend, Suffolk, England, grandson of Eva Carmichael.)

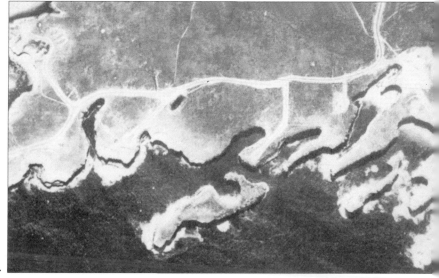

9.

Mutton Bird Island and the Loch Ard Gorge from the air. The wreck occurred off the lower tip of the island. Tom Pearce then Eva Carmichael were washed through the narrow entrance of the double-headed gorge. (Photograph by Department of Lands and Survey, Victoria.)

A contemporary artist's impression of the last moments of the *Loch Ard*. (From *Illustrated Sydney News*, 13th July 1878.)

12.

1.

One of the many photographs to appear of Tom Pearce in the weeks following the wreck. He was then aged eighteen. (By courtesy of the State Library of Victoria.)

Eva Carmichael some weeks after the wreck of the *Loch Ard*. She was eighteen when she lost her parents and five of her siblings. (By courtesy of the State Library of Victoria.)

The Loch Ard Gorge as it was until rock falls in the nineteen-forties obstructed the way to Eva Carmichael's Cave. The cave entrance may be seen at the right end of the beach. (From the A.W. Bennett Collection.)

13.

A 1970 photograph of the interior of Eva Carmichael's Cave. It runs back some seventy metres. (Photograph by Selwyn Duruz.)

14.

15.

This 1920s photograph of Glenample homestead shows the verandah added to it by Peter McArthur eight years after the wreck of the *Loch Ard*. (Photograph by Colin McArthur.)

16.
Hugh Gibson, who played a notable part in the rescue of Eva Carmichael from the Loch Ard Gorge. He lived at Glenample homestead with his wife, but operated the property in partnership with Peter McArthur. (By courtesy of the Warrnambool Library.)

17.
Stan McPhee, of Warrnambool, who located the remains of the *Loch Ard* in 1967. In 1973 with Ron Cashmore, another local man, he identified the wreck of the *Schomberg* near Peterborough. (By courtesy of Robert L. Suggett.)

18.
The ill-fated *Loch Ard* photographed at Gravesend in the Thames estuary. (By courtesy of the National Maritime Museum, Greenwich.)

19.

Pigs of lead plundered from the wreck of the *Loch Ard* two years after the wreck site was discovered. Those shown were seized by the police. (By courtesy of the *Warrnambool Standard*.)

20.

The Schomberg Reef. The *Schomberg* stranded on the landward side of its most prominent rock which is 350 yards from the nearest point to the beach. It appears that she was facing approximately west (left) toward the entrance to Curdies River. The larger part of the her hull lies half a mile east of this reef, a smaller part drifted to New Zealand. (Photo: courtesy Philip Adams.)

19
LAST VOYAGE

The *Loch Ard* left Gravesend on 2nd March 1878. The intention was to discharge cargo in Melbourne, then to return via the Horn with wool and wheat.

Quite apart from any ill name the *Loch Ard* may have gained as an unlucky ship, there were the usual causes, at least among the older passengers, for melancholy. Life in Britain might be impoverished and crowded for many, but at least it was familiar; and most of these passengers were not poor. The receding countryside had been tilled for generations into order and gentleness. At the journey's end lay a harsh, almost empty country where the seasons were strangely reversed and the familiar strata of society had become confused. In 1878, in Victoria, Ned Kelly formed a gang of bushrangers; in England Gilbert and Sullivan's *H.M.S. Pinafore* had its first production.

There was a song sailors sang as they worked in the rigging when long journeys began:

Our anchor's aweigh,
Our sails unfurled,
Good-bye, my love, good-bye.

The prospect of disaster must always have been in the minds of passengers and crew. Contemporary writers and illustrators did little to allay travellers' fears. In the year the *Loch Ard* sailed, an American poet, Bayard Taylor, died. *The Englishwoman's Domestic Magazine* had published, some years earlier, a poem of his side by side with its coloured illustrations of crinolines and bonnets; one can easily imagine the apprehensions it brought to those planning to emigrate:

The clouds are scudding across the moon;
  A misty light is on the sea;
The wind in the shrouds has a wintry tune,
  And the foam is flying free.

Brothers, a night of terror and gloom
  Speaks in the cloud and gathering roar;
Thank God, He has given us broad sea-room
  A thousand miles from shore.

Down with the hatches on those who sleep!
  The wild and whistling deck have we;
Good watch, my brothers, tonight we'll keep
  While the tempest is on the sea!

Though the rigging shriek in his terrbile grip,
  And the naked spars be snapped away,
Lashed to the helm, we'll drive our ship
  In the teeth of the whelming spray!

Hark! how the surges o'erlap the deck!
  Hark! how the pitiless tempest raves!
Ah! daylight will look upon many a wreck
  Drifting over the desert waves.

Yet, courage brothers! we trust the wave,
  With God above us, our guiding chart,
So, whether to harbour or ocean-grave,
  Be it still with a cheery heart.

When one considers that such descriptions were usually accompanied by dolorous illustrations, it is scarcely surprising that passengers did not always share the poet's cheery heart. But actualities were often every bit as bad as the conditions the poet described. One reads of a passage of the *Loch Awe*, when she reached Auckland from England in only sixty-nine days under a noted "hard driver", Captain Weir: "He drove her through everything, and the passengers were often battened down below; so that they were heartily glad to get to their destination." And if one did get there, there was scant prospect of saving enough money to return, even if one felt inclined to face such a voyage again.

The *Loch Ard* dropped the pilot at Start Point on 7th March. As he climbed down over the ship's side he carried with him last letters to those left behind. The dropping of the pilot was a severing of the umbilicus with the mother country. A life within a life lay ahead.

Relatively little is known of the *Loch Ard*'s voyage. The first section of the route to Australia took advantage of the northeast trade winds and the Canaries Current. As planned before the voyage, the *Loch Ard* sighted one of the Cape Verde Islands at approximately 15° N. 25° W. Then she moved south into the doldrums. It is evident that she emerged from this equatorial region much closer to South America than to Africa, for in latitude 12° 46′ S., longitude 30° 26′ W.— approximately five hundred miles east of Salvador—she was sighted by the *John Kerr*. Presumably this was the usual route, at any rate at that time of year, for the *John Kerr* was also Melbourne-bound—again the two ships that had shared the stormy 1874 arrival in Melbourne were together. They spoke on 9th April—thirty-eight days out for the *Loch Ard*, thirty-four for the *John Kerr*. Although they did not see each other again during the voyage, the two ships could not have moved far apart, for the *John Kerr* was to berth in Melbourne on 31st May, the day the *Loch Ard* approached Cape Otway.

The *Loch Ard* ran her easting down in latitudes from 40° S. to 42° S., a route taking her some five hundred miles south of the Cape of Good Hope. Soon after passing the Cape she ran before a half-gale under foresail and reefed upper topsails for several days, on some days logging over 335 miles—an average speed of nearly fourteen knots.

During the long days of the voyage Raby and Eva Carmichael learnt to take noon sun sights and work out the ship's position from them. As they gained proficiency their results differed little from those of the officers. At this distance in time it seems an incongruous picture: a heeling clipper in that loneliest of oceans; the two girls on the poop deck, sextants raised; Mama in all probability looking on from the deck below, not altogether approving of the attention of the officers. Raby and Eva appear to have been great favourites of the captain; their youth and their name must have taken his mind often to the bride he had left in England.

The marine sextant is a most accurate instrument, but, dependent as it is on reasonably clear skies and a defined horizon, it is of little use to a navigator if he approaches a coast in poor weather. This was to be Captain Gibb's problem as he neared his landfall. He had made a reasonably quick passage. On his ninetieth day at sea he was expecting to see Cape Otway. He had come up from the lonely reaches of the southern Indian Ocean to the gates of civilization—a remote, colonial civilization, he might have thought it, but one offering some of the comforts of home. Melbourne had by then a population of over a quarter of a million.

It was time for passengers to begin packing, to decide which London fashions to wear ashore, to look over letters of introduction—above all, time to watch for sight of land after three months in very restricted quarters in an often tumultuous sea.

The land expected was high and heavily forested; the first land in 9700 miles. Just how accurate the *Loch Ard*'s chronometer was is not known. The "daily rate" of gain or loss was determined before a chronometer was placed in a ship; thereafter it was checked at the end of each voyage. Though the daily rate was always known to navigating officers, there could be undetectable variations to it during a long voyage. Even if such variations amounted only to one second gained or lost each day, by the end of three months a navigating officer would be using data sufficiently erroneous to throw out his calculations of longitude by twenty or thirty miles. In an effort to cancel out variations to daily rate, three chronometers were often carried and a mean time was used. But whether the *Loch Ard* carried three is nowhere recorded.

On the night the *Loch Ard* approached the Otway-Wickham entrance to Bass Strait, Spong was still officer-in-charge of the Wickham light. During his fifteen years in the position, there had been fourteen major wrecks on the island, as well as wrecks of numerous coastal vessels. At Otway Ford was in his last year. He had already written to his superiors in Melbourne seeking release: "Sir, I hereby beg leave to inform you that I am now sixty years of age and that my health is fast failing. I

have been in charge of this Lighthouse nearly thirty years. . . .
I would most respectfully solicit that I may be allowed to retire
on superannuation."

Ford's son George had left the lighthouse and was working
on McArthur and Gibson's Glenample station, twenty-seven
miles west of Otway. This property was in undulating, desolate
country subject to frequent south-westerly gales. Over
thousands of years the prevailing winds have driven numerous
gorges into its soft limestone cliffs. So sheer and high are the
cliffs that there are few places where a survivor of shipwreck
could climb to safety.

Not far from Glenample homestead, six rock stacks rear out
of the sea, battered and eaten by waves, looking like remains of
tall ships. Farther west is the place now called Loch Ard Gorge,
and at its entrance is a tall island, rising as high as the mainland
cliffs. These are places that must have remained imprinted on
the young Ford's mind for the rest of his life.

20
THE WRECK

Captain Gibb expected to sight Cape Otway at 3 a.m. on 1st June. At noon on 31st May—the day the *John Kerr* berthed in Melbourne—Gibb's officers took their final meridian altitude of the sun in preparation for landfall. It was later described as a bad sight, presumably because the *Loch Ard* was running into conditions of poor visibility which later turned to thick haze on the landward side.

Until midnight Captain Gibb continued under full sail, then, approaching his landfall, he shortened sail and moved on slowly. As time passed without sign of the Otway light, he became concerned. He excused himself from an end-of-voyage celebration and remained with the officers of the watch.

Near Cape Otway the cliffs rise higher and change in formation and colour. They reach their highest point at Moonlight Head, so named by Matthew Flinders, who saw it when the moon emerged from behind cloud during a wild night on his 1802 *Investigator* voyage. This, at five hundred feet, is said to be the highest headland on the Australian mainland coast.

If one stands on the cliff-top at the Loch Ard Gorge, the great bulk of the headland obscures Cape Otway. So it was for Captain Gibb. Even had there been no haze, the Otway light would still have been screened from him, such was his undetected closeness to shore. To have seen the light he would have had to be at least four nautical miles out to sea; he was probably no more than three.

Had there been a watcher that night looking seaward from the cliffs twenty-seven miles west of Otway, he would have been looking into the same haze that restricted the vision of the crew of the *Loch Ard*. At 4 a.m. he would have seen the haze lift, leaving the night clear. At that moment he could scarcely have missed seeing a slow-moving clipper, spectre-like, alarmingly close to shore. Its immediate manoeuvres would have told the watcher that its master had begun a struggle with all odds against him.

On the *Loch Ard*, when the end-of-voyage party ended, Raby and Eva Carmichael walked the deck with Reginald Jones, a handsome young emigrant of twenty-seven who was going to Australia alone. Apparently his fiancée intended following him later. On his fingers he wore three rings, one engraved "Annie 19th October 1876". "Reg Jones had a foreboding of disaster," Eva Carmichael said later. "He often told me he had a pre-sentiment that he would never put foot on Victorian soil."

With Melbourne so close it is unlikely that many shared his fears. The girls were eagerly anticipating a first sight of land, but eventually they went to bed at midnight without a glimpse of it. Very soon they were asleep.

On the poop deck every man was straining for sight of Otway. At fifteen-minute intervals Captain Gibb sent a man aloft to watch for a break in the haze. Overhead the stars were clear and it was clear to seaward, but to the north there was nothing.

One of the men on watch was the apprentice Tom Pearce. Aged eighteen, he was only five feet five and a half inches tall, but compactly built and very fit. It was his third voyage on the *Loch Ard*. He had been to Calcutta under Captain Buchanan in 1876 and on the 1877 London–Melbourne–London voyage with Captain Mackay.

Born on 31st October 1859, Thomas Richard Pearce had gone to sea from his home in Melbourne at the age of fifteen. On 24th July 1875 he had sailed in the iron barque *Eliza Ramsden*, but his first voyage ended only hours after it had begun. The *Eliza Ramsden* struck the Corsair Rock at Port Phillip Heads. Fortunately all of her crew reached safety, but the ship was lost. Exactly four months before this Tom Pearce had lost his stepfather, Captain R. G. Pearce, master of the

Gothenberg, which was wrecked off the coast of north Queensland, between Townsville and Bowen, with the loss of a hundred and seven lives. Soon afterwards his mother had moved from Melbourne to San Francisco. Melbourne had been far from a happy city for her, for she had lost both her first and her second husband while living there.

At 4 a.m. Captain Gibb gave the order to heave the lead. It was at this moment that the haze lifted. About a mile ahead, indistinct in starlight, rose high, pale cliffs. The man aloft called that he could hear breakers. The crew must have realized immediately that their situation was desperate; they could only pin their hopes on the skill of Captain Gibb.

It was a situation Gibb had to meet entirely alone. It is scarcely possible today to appreciate fully the difficulties he faced. The twenty-eight sails of his vessel bore names that are now for the most part archaic; and one cannot readily understand the effect on the ship's speed and direction of the wide range of possible sail combinations. Consequently the purposes behind Gibb's decisions are largely lost to all but a few experts. One of these has recently said, "it was a copybook manoeuvre, perfectly carried out, but doomed from the beginning. He handled his heavy ship as one would handle a modern ocean racing yacht." The layman can more clearly appreciate the feelings of a man isolated by his authority, shouting his orders above the roar of the sea, a sea that was soon breaking right over his ship.

The *Loch Ard* had been running under topsails, jib and spanker on her slow approach to Cape Otway. When land was sighted only a mile off, Gibb ordered as much sail to be set as time allowed, then attempted to turn starboard out to sea. The ship swung round, but on coming head to wind her sails fell limp. She had not gathered enough impetus to carry her through the eye of the wind. Her head swung back to port.

Gibb then ordered both anchors to be let go—the move that saved the *Loch Ard* for Captain Green at the back of Sorrento on her maiden voyage. With each anchor went fifty fathoms of chain.

There were moments of waiting for the anchors to hold, then

it became evident that they were dragging over a smooth bottom. By this time the line of cliffs was only a half a mile off and the *Loch Ard* was in broken water. Behind her rose a tall island towards which she was drifting stern first.

The anchors at least had had the effect of bringing the ship's head back to the wind and swinging her stern away from the island. Captain Gibb ordered the yard-arms to be braced round to the port tack and the anchor cables to be slipped. He was about to attempt on this tack what he had first failed to do —to head out to sea.

Close though the ship was to the cliffs, this manoeuvre would probably have succeeded but for a reef running out from Mutton Bird Island. The mainsail alone was fully hauled and the wind was coming over the port beam when the ship struck the reef. So close was the ship to the island that her yard-arms struck its eastern cliff-face with each roll of the sea.

21
EVA CARMICHAEL

Below deck, Raby and Eva Carmichael had slept through the earlier part of the crisis. Wakened by shouts at four o'clock, they mistook the cries on deck for jubilation at the sighting of land. Eva put on her dressing-gown and hurried up the companionway. A din of waves met her and a scene of urgency and confusion. This was at the moment when Captain Gibb's first manoeuvre had failed. She returned quickly to the cabin. Raby, who was dressing, laughed unsuspectingly at her sister's eagerness to see land.

From her later account it is possible to reconstruct Eva's actions in the moments before the ship struck. No doubt she first told Raby of her fears, then one or the other of them went to wake those members of the family sleeping near by. At all events, there was sufficient time for Mrs Carmichael to get the small girls up and to begin dressing. Then the *Loch Ard* ran with a "fearful shuddering crash" onto the reef. So great was the impact that the whole of the top deck was loosened from the hull, and the masts and rigging began crashing across the ship. "The concussion was alarmingly loud and all was confusion and terror."

Below deck the first-class cabin space began flooding, for it was the after end of the ship that had struck the reef. Dr Carmichael and a steward got out six lifebelts from their stowage. These were fastened to Mrs Carmichael, to Raby, Eva, Mr and Mrs Stuckey, and to Dr Carmichael himself. But the strings kept breaking and they "had to be fastened anyhow".

Eva was seeing these members of her family for the last time. In the flooding cabin her two small sisters, Meta and Annie, were holding, crying, to their mother's dress and Mr. and Mrs. Stuckey were sitting on one of the seats still, "she clinging to her husband and crying". The brothers Evory and Thomas Carmichael, away in the second-class quarters, were not seen again.

Eva and Raby struggled up a companionway and made for Captain Gibb's post on the poop deck. "It was totally dark and impossible to see what was going on." It must have been evident enough, though, that the position was now hopeless. The deck itself was a shambles, for immediately the ship had struck the reef her topmast had come down, "striking in its passage two seamen and carrying them overboard, one appearing to be struck dead on the spot."

At the inquiry three weeks later it was said that the captain at once gave orders to get the lifeboats swung out and to have the women put into them, but the order could not be carried out because waves were breaking over the decks.

It is remarkable that the two girls reached Captain Gibb at all for he was on the port side of the poop deck to which they had to climb from the wave-swept main deck. He embraced Eva, "If you are saved, Eva, let my dear wife know that I died like a sailor". It was said of him later that he remained "cool, thoughtful and courageous amidst the general confusion and terror which prevailed".

High above them the girls saw streaks of light caused by one of the remaining yard-arms striking the cliffs of the island. At the same time tangled spars and large pieces of rock from the cliffs kept crashing on deck. Eva heard on of the stewards "praying loudly and asking God to save the souls of all aboard".

The *Loch Ard* was near her end. In the darkness distraught passengers and some of the crew were trying to shelter below deck from the falling rock and rigging. A wave larger than the rest swept Eva into the sea.

In the first moments in the water she thought she would perish of the intense cold. Struggling desperately, she was aware of cries and screams from those still on board. Raby was no longer with her, nor was she to see her again. Very soon, after hanging ten or fifteen minutes on the reef, the *Loch Ard* slipped off and disappeared into deep water. Only floating wreckage and struggling people were left in the waves. It was 5 a.m. and daylight was nearly two hours off.

22
TOM PEARCE

During the *Loch Ard*'s last moments Tom Pearce was trying to release a lifeboat with four others of the crew.

As the ship sank the wash of the sea from the cliff sent away the boat clear and capsized her. I was under the boat and must have remained there about three quarters of an hour. I got from under, but could see nobody, but a lot of floating wreckage. The tide was then ebb and carried the boat out to sea. When the flood made, the boat drifted in a little way. I got under again.

His account reveals a man well able to assess an emergency and decide upon the best course of action. His boat drifted eventually into a turbulent gorge only fifty yards across, shut between high cliffs. The swell, which outside rolled heavily, was compressed by this gorge and forced upward. It happened to right the boat and Pearce clambered into it. He was swept into the gorge, but part-way down it the boat struck a projecting cliff on the eastern side and he was thrown out again. It was now daylight and he saw that the gorge widened to a small beach on which wreckage was already piling. Abandoning the boat he struck out in calmer water for the beach. The swim through drifting wreckage proved a difficult one; by the time he reached the sand he was exhausted and his head was gashed badly. "When I got on shore I saw nothing of the ship or any of the people. I did not see the ship go down. I looked for a place of safety and got into a cave."

When the *Loch Ard* sank, Eva Carmichael was one of many people struggling in the sea near by. "One of the strings attached to my lifebelt broke and the belt, shifting up and down, forced my head under several times, which almost cost me my life. Seeing a hen-coop I swam towards it. God taught me to swim in my distressed plight for I had never swum before. I succeeded in reaching the hen-coop and so did Arthur Mitchell." She remembered afterwards saying to Mitchell, "So at last the despised hen-coops have some use!" All through the voyage they had been in the passengers' way.

By this time the ship had disappeared in the waves. Seeing a spar, I let go the hen coop and made for it. In a few minutes Mitchell and Jones were clinging to it also. Mitchell began to shiver frightfully and to despair of ever reaching the shore. He had a lifebelt, but poor Jones took off the life buoy which was around himself and put it round Mitchell. Mitchell asked me to give him some of my clothing to keep the wind from piercing him. I tried to do so, but could not divest myself of my jacket, having to hold on to the spar with one hand. Poor Jones and Mitchell soon let go the spar, and after swimming some little distance, disappeared, and I saw them no more.

The fact that Eva Carmichael could not swim and so could only cling to the spar undoubtedly saved her life, for the spar kept outside the line of breakers on the island and after several hours drifted into the gorge through which Pearce had passed about an hour earlier.

Clinging tenaciously to her spar and her life, she was probably only vaguely aware of her surroundings. It was perhaps as well. A few days later the Melbourne *Argus* was to describe the place: "The coast for miles to eastward and westward shows nothing but precipitous rocks rising perpendicularly from the water to heights varying from a hundred and fifty feet to three hundred feet and it is only at intervals of many miles that there is an inlet or gorge through the rocks where there is a small beach on which a landing can be effected."

Such was the gorge into which Eva Carmichael had been thrown by the waves. "The cliff rises straight out of the sea to a height of about a hundred and fifty feet," said the *Argus*, "without a single ledge on which a bird could rest."

Soon after she was flung through the entrance of the gorge, Eva Carmichael's spar jammed against the same projecting cliff that Pearce's boat had struck and her clothing caught on a rock. By now she could intermittently see what appeared to her to be a rocky shore, then a man walking among the rocks. She screamed to him for help.

The "rocks" were in actuality pieces of wreckage from the *Loch Ard*. Pearce was looking among them for food. When first he heard her he thought someone was calling him from the cliff-top, but on hearing the voice a second time he saw the girl struggling about midway up the gorge. Although weak from his own struggle and from loss of blood, he threw off most of his remaining clothing and began swimming to her in a heavy sea that was "lashing upon piles of wreckage and tossing them wildly in all directions".

When he reached her she was still clinging to the spar that had so far saved her. To his dismay she lost consciousness and he had difficulty in breaking her grip. Pulling her free, he caught her nightgown in his teeth and tried to drag her through the wreckage. Providentially an upturned table drifted near him. Grasping this, he was able to make better progress. Intermittently the girl must have regained consciousness, for she said later, "Tom had a desperate struggle to bring me ashore. From the time I shouted to him up to the time we were safe on the beach, must have been an hour."

Her recollections of happenings on the beach were clearer. "He took me into a wild-looking cave a few hundred feet from the beach and finding a case of brandy, broke a bottle and made me swallow some, which revived me. He pulled some long grass and shrubs for me to lie on. I soon sank into a state of unconsciousness and must have remained so for hours. We must have been fully five hours in the water."

Some days later a reporter of the *Illustrated Sydney News* wrote, "I am inclined to believe that the lady still retained her consciousness until she was brought into the cave, for I do not consider it possible for Mr Pearce (strong and active though he is) to have carried her across the wreckage by his own unaided effort."

23
THE GORGE

At its nearest point, the elongated Mutton Bird Island is only about fifty yards from shore. Today, across this gulf, tourists watch at dusk in summer for whirling clouds of mutton birds (short-tailed shearwater) returning to their young on the island. But the *Loch Ard*'s actual point of impact was about six hundred yards from the mouth of the gorge, so, even if the two survivors had drifted directly in, they would have come half a mile. But, as Pearce stated, the tide had taken him out to sea then back again. Undoubtedly they drifted considerably further.

Standing on the cliff-tops at this place one may see the waves approaching the coast in long parallel lines, as many as twenty at a time, each advancing steadily behind the last. Close in, they break on reefs and against strange, tall islands and under arches. The landward end of Mutton Bird Island itself forms a high arch. All this is carved from the limestone of which the coast there consists—a tawny stone, iron-streaked here and there by oozing water. The waves rush forward as if to devour the whole country. They leap at the cliffs, but fall back in rivulets to the white mass of broken water. All this action is accompanied by a vast range of sounds, as if the sea were at once shouting exultant threats and groaning in defeat.

Seen from above, the gorge is not unlike the letter Y, the long arm being the entrance from the sea. In the right or eastern arm is a cave called today Tom Pearce's Cave—a miserable place, with a floor of rock and a constant dripping of water. A small stream flows out of it and loses itself in the sand. Although this is supposed traditionally to be the cave where Pearce first rested, his own evidence suggests that he searched out a second, less accessible cave that afforded him protection from the wind. This is in the western arm of the gorge. Certainly this was the cave to which he later "half carried, half dragged" Miss Carmichael. This is confirmed by an entry in the diary of that great adventurer "Chinese" Morrison who, as a Geelong College schoolboy, visited the gorge while staying at Glenample nineteen months after the wreck—he was on a lone walk from Geelong to Adelaide by the coast. "The celebrated cave . . . is just around the first corner to the W. arriving in from the sea. It runs out in the direction of the sea for a distance of 75 yards." With the passage of years its entrance has become partially blocked by falls of rock, and today it is cut off by shallow water at high tide. One can only suppose that the pruderies of the time dictated need for separate caves for the young survivors, despite their circum-stances, for this cave is segregated by name as "Eva Carmichael's Cave". At the time of the wreck and for many years afterwards a clear stretch of sand led to the entrance, but this has long since been scoured out. Facing north-east as it does, it offers shelter from the wind and, inside, the floor is sandy. A few paces into it takes one into semi-darkness.

To Tom Pearce, looking up at the vertical walls of the gorge, the place must have seemed like a prison yard. They were walls he had now to find a way of climbing. Shut in down there, the sound of the sea was reduced to a thud and drone of waves outside the entrance.

Pearce said afterwards that he had made Eva Carmichael drink half a bottle of brandy he had found among the wreckage and that he had finished the bottle himself. This was probably something of an overstatement, for he also mentioned using some of the brandy to rub on her body. However much he gave her, he was undoubtedly right in saying, "I am sure it saved her life, although it put her in a stupor from which I could not wake her [when] I left her to look for help." Nor did he himself get far at first on his search.

After drinking so much brandy I began to feel very drowsy and went to find as sheltered spot as I could and laid down. I must have slept for some time. When I woke I had a good look amongst the wreckage which was piled on the beach to see if anybody had been washed ashore, but found no one. As the day was very cloudy, I had not much idea of the time, but it must have been well after midday when I made the attempt to climb the cliffs to see if there were any houses in sight.

So many years after the event it is difficult to determine from his own account where Tom Pearce climbed out, but "Chinese" Morrison's diary is fairly explicit. The headland to which the diary refers juts into the gorge from the landward side, dividing it into its two arms. "The beach [of the gorge]," says Morrison, "is accessible only by means of steps cut down the headland into the W. gorge and it was at the extremity of the headland, also on the W., that Tom Pearce scaled." This refers to two places: the steps and the place where Pearce scaled, which is at the "extremity of the headland". It would appear from this that he did not see the steps, probably because of the thick scrub that filled the whole western arm of the gorge, but that they were already there is evidenced by the relatively easy descent in darkness of the rescuers. That Pearce did not climb out at the first attempt, even though he was undoubtedly a nimble climber, is evident from his story. Today the climb is relatively easy, as sand has formed a virtual ramp in the western arm and much of the scrub has gone. The primitive steps probably followed an earlier Aboriginal track, for it is evident that there was an age-old midden at the top. The modern steps descend from this midden and follow the old descent.

"When I got to the top," said Pearce, "my heart sank, as I could not see anything that indicated any settlement. The thought of Miss Carmichael lying in that cave made me make the effort to get help, so I started along the coast, but having no boots on, progress was slow."

Inland were low desolate hills; along the cliff-tops she-oak grew thickly. The likelihood of finding help appeared remote. Pearce began walking westward. He could not know that he was only three and a half miles west of McArthur and Gibson's Glenample station homestead and was walking away from it.

24
TO GLENAMPLE

At Glenample George Ford was working that Saturday afternoon with a fourteen-year-old boy, William Till, mustering sheep. Providentially Pearce came upon the hoof-prints of their horses. The *Warrnambool Standard* relates the ensuing happenings:

Ford was mustering sheep when he observed a boy walking near the edge of the cliff and in riding up to him and seeing he was much scarred asked him what was the matter. The boy reported that the *Loch Ard* was lost, with all on board, passengers, captain and crew, except himself and a girl whom he had assisted to rescue. . . . The boy indicated to Ford from the beach the spot where the vessel went down, but he did not see anything of her at the time owing to the height of the cliffs. The boy, Thomas Pearson [*sic*] then went back to the beach where he had left the young lady, and Ford rode back to McArthur and Gibson's station to procure help.

The report did not mention William Till, but it was Till who recalled afterwards the cut on the side of Pearce's head and his anxiety for Eva Carmichael. Exhausted as she was, and with only her nightgown left her, Pearce was afraid that exposure to the winter night would be the end of her.

When the men brought their news to Glenample, Hugh Gibson, part-owner and manager of the station, was sceptical; indeed scepticism seems to have been part of his nature, but so also were resourcefulness and determination and generosity. Admittedly Ford's story of a shipwrecked youth with bleeding hands and feet, and smelling strongly of brandy, sounded improbable. But "Mrs Gibson persuaded her husband that it could be true, for a wandering drunk would hardly be so far from habitation". On deciding to investigate, Gibson thought it prudent to say as little as possible about a wreck among his men, since he realized that sightseers and looters would swarm across the country, however rough and lonely it was.

In the meantime Pearce had descended back into the gorge, probably by the steps which would have been evident from the top. Gibson was not long after Pearce, but it was by then dark; next came Ford. They found that the girl had gone from the cave where Pearce had left her.

The gorge was not large, but there were numerous places, especially in the dense scrub, where a person could lie concealed. The men searched in the dark, coo-eeing urgently. They were still searching when Tom Pearce collapsed. Gibson covered him with a blanket, remarking, "Let him rest—he's dead beat."

William Till was sent back to Glenample for lanterns and the buggy and for more men. Some years later he wrote:

When I got back to the house I delivered my message and the men—Mr. W. Robertson, of Port Campbell, Mr. Shields of Princetown (riding) and Mr. McKenzie, senior, of Glenample with a boy driving a buggy, returned. By the time we arrived back at the wreck it would be about ten o'clock p.m. Mr. Robertson called out from the top of the cliff, and almost at the same instant Ford called out from below, "I have found her." As Robertson scrambled down the cliff, Ford was in the act of removing Miss Carmichael from under a bush. She was quite helpless and had to be lifted up and was unable to speak. Soon a good fire was got going with the piles of wreckage on the beach and Miss Carmichael soon recovered and was able to take a cup of coffee. Pearce was then aroused and brought to the fire, and after he was given something to eat.

Till remembered that the girl's arms had been blue with bruises. Her first words were, "Where is Tom Pearce?"

Several days passed before Eva herself was able to tell what had happened after Pearce had left her in the cave.

When I woke up I felt very confused and very sore all over, but after awhile I began to recollect things very clearly and got up to find Tom Pearce. When I got out of the cave I could not see him anywhere. I did not know what had become of him. Before I left England I heard so much about the wild blacks which were out here and I thought the ship had struck against an island that was peopled with blacks, so, before it got dark, I went and crawled under the thickest bush I could find in the gorge. I heard something that sounded like "coo-ee", and when I heard that strange call I thought I was amongst the blacks and kept concealed.

But then she heard someone say one word—"Yes". Her account continues:

I thanked God when I heard that English word, and was instantly in the company of Mr. Gibson and that young man George Ford. Mr Gibson took off his shoes and stockings and put them on me, and wrapped me in blankets. A fire was soon made, and coffee boiled and brandy produced. I felt my strength somewhat recruited, but for all that felt weak and helpless, and sore with the bruises received from the rocks and floating wreckage. Mr Gibson kindly wrapped me in warm clothing. In the darkness of the night a young man named William Robertson, of Port Campbell, and William Shields, under the superintendence of Mr Gibson, conveyed me up the steep and lofty precipice. I cannot understand how they succeeded in bringing me to the top. It must have been a work of great difficulty and danger.

"It was a good thing," wrote William Till in his account, "that we had two such hefty men as W. Robertson and W. Shields, otherwise she would not have seen the top of the cliff that night."

Eva Carmichael spoke to William Shields before they brought her up out of the gorge. Finding that she came from Dublin, Shields said, "I have an uncle who is a druggist there." "Is it Cunningham's?" the girl asked. It was. Dr Carmichael had often had prescriptions made up there. Shields's mother had been a Cunningham. It was a strange coincidence in such sadly contrasting circumstances.

Till's account continued:

There being no track, Mr Robertson led the horse in the buggy home, arriving at Glenample house between 3 and 4 a.m., so that Miss Carmichael, from the time the ship struck until she was safe in bed again, was over 20 hours in the open. During most of that period she only had her night-dress on. Before 11 a.m. on Sunday the authorities had news of the wreck in Melbourne, thanks to the hard riding of G. Ford.

In the cave, by candlelight, Hugh Gibson had drafted a telegram to the Commissioner of Customs and a note to the police officer at Camperdown and had given these scraps of paper to George Ford to deliver. Two hours after Miss Carmichael was found, Ford left to ride forty-five miles over a rough and hilly track to Camperdown. Word had to go not only to the agents of the *Loch Ard* but eventually to the unsuspecting relatives of her passengers and crew. Ford's ride must be counted as one of the outstanding feats of horsemanship in early Victoria. On a horse that he had ridden all day, he covered a total of ninety miles, half of it in darkness.

The telegram from Gibson to the Commissioner of Customs at Melbourne was lodged at Camperdown at 9 a.m. on Sunday, 2nd June: "The ship *Loch Ard* was wrecked off this coast last night. All hands and passengers are supposed to be lost, except Miss Evaline Carmichael and Tom Pearce (midshipman) who swam ashore. The place of the wreck is about one mile east from the Sherbrooke. I hope protection will be given from wreckers."

When this news was known in Melbourne all ships in port flew their flags at half mast. In the meantime help was sent from Camperdown, as related by the *Camperdown Standard*:

Intelligence was brought to Camperdown this morning by George Ford, one of the employees on McArthur and Gibson's Glenample station, about fifty miles to the south of this, of the wreck of the *Loch Ard*. . . . Ford, who arrived at Camperdown at about 8 o'clock [Sunday morning] . . . left at about 10 o'clock with Mounted Trooper Graham to render what further assistance they could and to take charge of such portions of the wreck as might be washed on shore.

The *Standard* then gave Ford's account of the search for the missing girl, ending with the words, "Evaline Carmichael is deadly pale and ill."

25
HUGH GIBSON

Glenample was first settled by James Murray in 1855—the year the *Schomberg* was wrecked twelve miles to the west. In 1866 Murray sold it to the partners McArthur and Gibson. Hugh Gibson it was who built a homestead of sandstone quarried within a mile of the site—the cliffs change from limestone to sandstone not far east of the homestead. There he lived with his rather delicate wife, Lavinia. Born in Scotland in 1830, Gibson had come out to Australia at the age of seventeen. At the time of the wreck of the *Loch Ard* he was forty-eight. His partner, Peter McArthur, lived eight miles north-west of Camperdown on his property Meningoort; this put him about fifty miles from Glenample.

In the words of a man who stayed at Glenample in later years, it was "rather a plain building" with "a wide verandah around it. At the back, and attached to the main building, were a kitchen, storerooms and other rooms." It faced east and the front rooms were warmed by the morning sun. Although protected from the full force of the south-westerly gales by a grassy hill lying between it and the coast, its trees and shrubs were nevertheless pressed inland by the winds.

Of the many accounts describing happenings following the wreck of the *Loch Ard*, Hugh Gibson's own, written in a letter to his stepmother, while Eva Carmichael and Tom Pearce were still at Glenample, is the most vivid:

MY DEAR MOTHER,
    Your kind letter should have been answered before, but as Lavinia is very busy, and is also suffering in her hand, I am doing it for her.

No doubt the escape of Miss Carmichael and Tom was most miraculous and much more so than people think. I feel perfectly that it was Providence that favoured them, and also the same Power that kept Lavinia and me from going to Berta's wedding, as if we had been absent from home, I think it exceedingly probable that the search for Eva would have been abandoned until daylight, in which case she would scarcely have recovered, if found alive.

The reports in the papers were very varied, and had I known that there was going to be such a fuss about it I would have written a full and particular account myself.

It was while mustering sheep at the home yards that I met George Ford (about sundown) and he told me about meeting Pearce. I was inclined not to believe it, but when he told me about the young lady I told them to go on and get the sheep in whilst I went to Lavinia and told her to get some food and drink ready, but not to tell a soul. I then, after instructing George and the boy Willie who was with him, to follow me and to bring a blanket apiece, rode off and never pulled rein until I had got above the Caves Gorge. It was then so dark that I could not tell there was wreckage beneath, although there was a barrier of it at least 8 ft. high from one side of the beach to the other. I cooeyed several times, but got no answer and was uncertain if Tom had described the place properly, or whether he had succeeded in finding the spot again.

However I went down and whilst fairly at the bottom I cooeyed again and got an answer from Tom to the effect that he was fast in the scrub; he was barefooted and in a nasty place. I got him out and we at once went to the cave where Eva had been left—saw the grass bed he had made for her, but no Eva. Tom and I went round the cave again and again, then over to the other cave, still no sign of her. I then commenced to try and track her, but could only see Tom's track up and his own returning again. This must have taken an hour, when George and Willie arrived, and finding some candles we made lanterns with bottles and commenced the search over again. I then determined to send for proper lanterns and to get all hands so as not to leave a stone unturned.

Whilst the boy was away Ford and I sat down regularly puzzled. I made Tom lie down and he went to sleep. After waiting what appeared to us two hours, we began to think that the people could not find the place as it was pitch dark, so I told Ford to go up and light a fire on the top to guide them, and when half way up he heard the voice, "I'm dying", when we sprung into where she was at once. She was in a regular hole covered with scrub, and must have crawled in. She had no recollection of leaving the cave, but I am convinced that she must actually have walked in Tom's footprints prompted by some instinct or other. When I first saw her I certainly thought she was insane. She had only half a stocking on one leg and very little clothing although sufficient to screen her person. We at once rolled her in blankets. I put my sock and shoes on her and let her lie, thinking she would get warm, but after a while she complained of being chilled, so I got a rousing fire made of wreck timber to which we took her and by that means got her so that she was enabled to get up the cliffs with assistance. . . . The Place where we found her was within 5 yards of where I got Tom fast in the scrub and she must have then been insensible otherwise she must have heard us talking. I think she displayed as much pluck and bravery as Tom. Her story was told at the very first and no doubt she encouraged Jones and Mitchell who were on the same spar. She tried to get her skirt off for Mitchell, who was naked and complained of cold, but failed. She must have been in the water for more than an hour longer than Tom, as she came in on a small spar which did not present any surface for the wind to help it on, whereas Tom had the lifeboat which would float very high.

Lavinia will post you a pencil sketch of the Gorge and she will likely tell you more at some future day.

Further sections of this letter have more relevance to a later chapter and will be quoted there. Twenty-eight years after these events, when Hugh Gibson was a man of seventy-six and Lavinia was dead, he enlarged on this account. He recalled then that while they were searching they were sometimes "walking on the keyboards of pianos that had been broken from their cases". He goes on:

The newspapers had it that my cooeying had frightened her. But this was not the case with Miss Carmichael, as I found her within three yards of where I had found Pearce in the scrub, and if she was not insensible or asleep, she *must* have heard us talking.

Even after such a passage of years, Hugh Gibson is clearly puzzled by the girl's silence. A conjecture made years afterwards by an unidentified journalist of the *Australasian* may well be close to the truth:

. . . the poor girl had been swept from the wreck clad only in her night dress and in 1878 women were not sufficiently emancipated to bear with equanimity a display of limb such as fashion sanctions in 1928. There is no doubt that, waking in such piteous circumstances—alone, half naked and on an unknown shore—her first thought was flight and concealment. Her rescuers said that when found at nightfall she was crouched among the bushes and wrapped about with twisted twigs and boughs.

This conjecture strikes one as similar to Hugh Gibson's remark to his stepmother: "She had . . . very little clothing although sufficient to screen her person." While standards of decency and indecency change from generation to generation and we are all at the mercy of whatever standard happens to prevail in our time, one is dismayed when modesty is not suspended in the face of such tragedy and such peril to a survivor.

Gibson's later account ends:

After Ford left, as it was now midnight, I thought that we had better make a start and get home; so, by pulling and pushing, we got Miss Carmichael up to the top, and into the buggy. Pearce and I were the other passengers. With the lad leading the horse by means of a lantern, we reached Glenample at about 2 a.m.

26
THE DEAD

Hugh Gibson's later account moves now into the days immediately following the wreck:

I went down next morning at daylight and found a great accumulation of wreckage. The beach at the gorge I would say was 300 yards long from cliff to cliff, and there was a barricade at least eight feet high, right across, consisting of ship's cargo, which comprised commodities of all descriptions. You could not name an article of commerce that was not there. The barrier of wreckage contained goods of every conceivable description. There were pianos, concertinas, piece goods, ladies' dresses, candles, brandy and spirits, champagne, strychnine, telegraph instruments, etc. These were all at the foot of a gorge accessible only at one spot, and so, to a certain extent, secure from wreckers. I did not stay long that morning as there was only one harmless man there, a local resident. As for the ship, she was out of sight many fathoms deep, but there was a piece of spar hanging on the base of the cliff, with the reflection of sail below the water that marked the place where she had foundered. She was lost on an inaccessible island close to the mainland. . . . I went down again in the afternoon, and then found Mrs and Miss Raby Carmichael, who had been washed ashore with lifebelts on, and pulled them above high water mark, covering them with calico we found among the wreckage. They were fully clothed and had not a scratch on them.

I went down again on Monday morning. By this time, people were arriving, and during the forenoon we found the bodies of Jones and Mitchell floating amongst the wreckage. They were in a nude state, but not at all bruised, which was a wonder, as they were amongst heavy wreckage. We got them ashore, and placed them along-side the bodies. Police arrived. Mr Foster, a visitor at Tandarook, who came down, volunteered to make coffins. [Tandarook, near Camperdown, was the property of Dr Daniel Curdie, a well-known early settler.]

On Tuesday the crowd got larger. I should say that there were not fewer than 400 people. Captain Daish, agent for the underwriters, and young Mr Blyth, representing the agents of the ship, came. These latter came in a very unprepared state. I had to provide them with tarpaulins for tents, and rope, and tools.

Press representatives from Melbourne and Sydney and from the smaller towns were quickly on the scene. Their reports confirm one's impression that adequate protection against wreckers was not sent. All manner of sightseers and undesirables were flocking to the gorge. Some were caught making off with valuables by the cartload; others succeeded in getting clear away. The *Illustrated Sydney News* wrote:

At the Sherbrook River there is an open beach about half a mile long, on which much of the cargo was washed ashore, consisting principally of broken harmoniums and numberless cases of wax vesta; also a large quantity of furniture, table tops, and other articles, but these were speedily removed by persons who came down from Port Campbell, Scott's Creek and other places with carts and pack horses. It is a well-known fact that hundreds of pounds worth of goods have been conveyed away by people who honestly believed they had a perfect right to all they could lay hands upon, provided the police did not catch them. A case of toys and another of Birmingham jewellery found their way up to Cowley's Creek, and in any of the houses there a stranger may see some of the articles amusing the children, or adorning the females. In one house, I was shown a young gentleman elegantly attired in an overcoat of which he is very proud, but which I had reason to know for certain had been purloined from a reporter of one of the newspapers, who had incautiously left it on the cliff while he was taking notes on the beach below.

On the western side of the caves gorge, there is another inlet where much of the cargo lies, but this, being near the police camp, has been, so far as I know, untouched. A little further on, however, there is about twelve yards of beach, to which the wreckers resorted nightly. I observed the grass all trodden down at the edge of the cliffs, and a strong stake driven in by which the thieves are lowered to the wreckage. Their footmarks are distinctly visible on the sand below.

Gibson had hoped that the lighthouse supply ship, *Pharos*, would be sent quickly to sweep the various beaches and bays in case survivors had reached shore but were trapped at the foot of the cliffs. This was a distinct possibility. But the *Pharos* was never sent; indeed, it is doubtful whether such a search would have been practicable in so dangerous an area.

Tom Pearce accompanied Hugh Gibson the morning after the wreck. Only he could identify the recovered bodies. Gibson wrote:

On Wednesday the coffins were ready. The next thing was to get the bodies up the cliff, which was an undertaking. For that purpose I had an open shell made in which we placed them, one at a time, and, securing it so that there was no danger of the remains falling out, got them hoisted by willing hands from above. I superintended the operation, and got it finished without a hitch. On reaching the top they were put into their separate coffins, Mrs McArthur and Mrs Gibson cutting off locks of hair for relatives.

McArthur held a magisterial inquiry at which Pearce gave evidence of identity, and I to the finding.

Peter McArthur was a Justice of the Peace. "I am of the opinion," he recorded, "that owing to the weak state of Miss Evaline Carmichael, one of the two survivors of the wreck, it would be inadvisable to subject her to any examination."

His papers were headed: "Report of an enquiry held before me, one of her Majesty's Justices of the Peace for the Colony of Victoria at the scene of the wreck of the ship *Loch Ard* on 5th June 1878 on the bodies of Reginald Jones, Arthur Mitchell, Mrs Carmichael and Miss Rebecca Carmichael."

Pearce, after formally identifying the bodies stated: "I believe them to have been drowned between 5 and 6 a.m. on Saturday last."

Gibson next gave evidence. He spoke of Ford's discovery of "a young man with his head split open" and of the subsequent search for Miss Carmichael.

Last to give evidence was Constable Robert Graham of Camperdown. Telling of his inspection of the gorge the day after the wreck, he said, "I saw two bodies lying on the shore since identified as those of Mrs Carmichael and Miss Carmichael. . . . On the following day I saw another body in the surf—I had it brought ashore—since identified as that of

Reginald Jones. . . . On the following day saw another body in the surf—I had it brought ashore—since identified as that of Arthur Mitchell."

One of the newspapers remarked on Jones's "three valuable rings".

These were nearly falling prey to the rapacity of a wrecker, whose assumed respectability would have led to the belief that the dead were safe from sacrilege at his hands. They were not so, however, and the despoiler had to disgorge his ill-gotten possessions. One of the rings, it is said, was a present from the young lady to whom Mr Jones was engaged in the old country, and Miss Carmichael (to whom Jones appears to have confided some of his private affairs) has expressed a wish to forward it to his bereaved fiancée.

The graves were dug at the top of the cliffs, little more than a hundred yards from the place where Eva Carmichael and Tom Pearce had reached shore. Initials and ages were cut deeply into the lids of coffins made of piano cases brought up from the wreckage.

Shortly before the burial service began, a gold watch was found under Mrs Carmichael's waistband. Eva later identified it as her father's. It had been made by a Dublin watchmaker for George IV; the King had failed to send for it and subsequently her father had bought it for a hundred guineas.

Even though the place was remote and sparsely populated, a large crowd attended the funeral. The service was conducted by I. Keith McIntyre, Presbyterian Bush Missionary of the Heytesbury Forest district. "Mr McIntyre read portion of the 15th Chapter of the 1st Corinthians, and delivered a short address from the words, 'And the sea gave up the dead which were in it' (Revelations 20 Verse 13). The service was most impressive."

In that windswept place directly above the gorge, with the background of the sea, it could scarcely have been otherwise. But during the solemnities there was a bizarre interruption. For its understanding it is necessary to remark that Eva Carmichael had already told those at Glenample something of her antecedents: "Her late mother was a Plantagenet, a descendant of Henry VII . . . she is related to some of the Irish Nobility."

Perhaps because he had seen the ladies of Glenample cut locks from the hair of the deceased women, "a Scotchman who seemed to have a 'wee drap in his ee' said to his companions, 'Here lies royal bluid, ma frien'. We dinna drap across a Plantagenet every day; sae, let's jist tak a wee pickle o' her hair, by way o' a keepsake, ye ken.' Whereupon they cut a small portion of her hair, reverentially wrapped it up in a paper, and seriously walked off with their treasure."

Presumably the other Scots present were shocked into immobility.

Hugh Gibson later erected over the grave a cross of spars from the wreckage.

27
THE AFTERMATH

"The people that came (to Glenample) stayed for days," said Gibson. "How they lived I do not know. In my men's hut, which was not a large one, I have gone at night and found one hundred sleeping all over the floor. I had representatives of the *Argus*, *Age*, *Herald* and *Warrnambool Standard* sleeping on the floor of my dining-room before the fire, as you may say all under the same blanket, and they did not fall out."

Keith McIntyre stayed at Glenample for three days. On each of these evenings he conducted services at the homestead. According to the *Argus* reporter this was customary on the missionary's visits there.

All the employees and visitors were present. The service was a short one consisting only of two Moody and Sankey hymns, the reading of a chapter from the New Testament and extempore prayer. The singing was accompanied by Mrs Gibson on the piano and both Miss Carmichael and Thomas Pearce were present and evidently took great interest in the earnest prayer offered up on behalf of those who were lost, and those who were saved from the terrible disaster.

It was to McIntyre that Eva Carmichael gave her account of the wreck and of her mother's link with the Plantagenets. This account was included in *A Narrative of the Wreck of the Ship Loch Ard*, compiled in 1890 by Richard Bennett.

Work at Glenample was paralysed, not only because of the task of nursing Eva Carmichael, but because the search for bodies and the protection of wreckage had to continue and Glenample remained the centre of activity.

Some days after the wreck a fifth body was found. Gibson

recorded that "Pearce identified [it] as young Rolleston, son of a clergyman, of Cornwall. . . . His remains we were obliged to bury where found as we could not remove them." It is not known where this was.

The *Warrnambool Standard* reported that two more bodies were seen in a gorge below Glenample homestead, "but the risk is too great to secure them, the sides being over two hundred feet high and perfectly straight, whilst the swell and backwash would render attempts to recover the dead too great a risk to the living".

The *Argus* reported that "three or four bodies had been seen floating in different inlets". A group of men went eastward along the coast to see if it would be possible to recover them for burial.

Upon reaching the first inlet a close examination was made of the waves which were dashing in against precipitous cliffs. After a time the body of a stout-built man was seen among the breakers; but it was impossible to recover it, as the cliffs there were about 200 ft. high and went straight down into the water without giving any foothold for a man. The body, from the description given by Pearce, was thought to be one of the seamen. Proceeding to the next inlet running in from Elephant Island another body was seen in the water. At the head of this inlet was a small sandy beach, over which the water rolled pretty frequently, and as the body at the time lodged among the rocks, some of those present thought it might be recovered and buried. It appeared to be that of a middle-sized man, with dark hair. Only one leg remained, but as there was a wellington or sea boot on that leg, it was supposed to be also one of the seamen. There were two men present who were quite ready to go down the cliff and attempt to recover the body if they were paid to do so. The Government officials present thought, and perhaps very properly, that they had no right to offer monetary inducement to men to risk their lives in order to recover a dead body, and would not, therefore promise any money to a man to go down. Seeing that they were obstinate, an elderly man named Lengabeer, but locally known as "Robinson Crusoe" in consequence of his dress, decided to go, trusting to the Government to pay him for his risk afterwards. A rope was obtained, and taking a sack in his hand to bring the body up in, he fastened a bowline round his waist, and was lowered down over the cliff, which was there about 180 ft. high. By the time this was arranged and he was lowered down to the beach, the undertow of the current had taken the body out seawards, and it was tossing about in the surf. The man remained down on the beach for some little time, but as he found that the sea was increasing, and there was no possibility of obtaining the body, the attempt had to be given up, and the people on top of the cliff hauled the man up. The attempt was a plucky one, but it appears that this is not the first time the same man has risked his life.

For grisly detail the *Illustrated Sydney News* report outdid all others:

The dead bodies have drifted into the bights and indentations west of Pearce Inlet, and all present a mutilated appearance. One stout-built baldheaded man is believed to be Dr Carmichael, while another is evidently that of a sailor who was transfixed by a falling mast, as a portion of his bowels are protruding from the back. These bodies present a dreadful sight as they are tossed to and fro by the heavy surf; the rags still clinging to them give them the appearance of stuffed figures most horrible to look upon. The body of a female is conjectured to be that of Mrs Stuckey, as she was the only lady with fair hair on board the unfortunate vessel. A man from town has been living on the coast for some days engaged in looking out for the corpses of Mr and Mrs Stuckey and in all weathers he may be seen religiously carrying out his instructions.

This was a diver named Erickson who, having been employed by relatives of the Stuckeys, arrived at the gorge with two coffins in a dray.

On 10th June representatives of a company interested in salvage rights to the *Loch Ard* repaired the lifeboat to which Tom Pearce had clung. The day being calm, they rowed out through the gorge until they were over the site of the wreck. They concluded that on calm days divers would be able to work on it. They rowed then to the other side of Mutton Bird Island, and there, on a beach scarcely fifty yards long, they found Mrs Stuckey's remains. As the tide was coming in, their situation was fast becoming dangerous. They could do no more than scrape a grave with their hands.

The *Illustrated Sydney News* reported bodies seen in the near-by blowhole, from which it was impossible to recover them:

The entrance to this cannot be observed from the land, but about five hundred yards inland among the scrub there is a huge hole about fifty yards long by twenty wide, with sides running vertically down to a depth of about sixty feet. Here the sea rushes in with terrific force through the channel connecting it with the ocean, and after spending its fury against the rocky sides of the hole, passes on through another cave which penetrates further inland, but to what extent it is impossible to estimate.

It is claimed in the late Margaret MacKenzie's *Shipwrecks*, that in the Blowhole eleven bodies were counted and that by night the hole glowed with a mauve light caused by vestas from the cargo. The claim is undoubtedly correct, for Mrs MacKenzie's father, Charles McGillivray, was on the scene for many days after the wreck, having been placed in charge of wreckage until representatives of the underwriters arrived.

The underwriters' most immediate task was to determine how much of value could be salvaged. Their representative, Captain Joseph Daish, arrived on the Tuesday after the wreck. He first obtained a declaration from Tom Pearce and incorporated this in his statement:

The ship "Loch Ard" sailed from London on 1st March 1878 on a Voyage to Melbourne laden with a Cargo of General Merchandise. They proceeded on the voyage and experienced fine weather and at times strong variable winds with occasional fresh gales.

That on the 30th and 31st May they had thick hazy weather the sky being completely overcast, so much so that on neither of those two days could the Captain obtain an observation of the sun. On Saturday the following morning being the 1st June the ship was running with the wind well on her beam under close reefed topsails when at about 4 a.m. the Captain who was on deck at the time saw the land and breakers about half a mile ahead. The Captain at once gave orders to haul the ship's head to the wind, but the vessel would not stay and being close in shore she could not weather the land, they then let go both anchors with 50 fathoms of cable on each; but they did not succeed in bringing the vessel up, and she continued to drag towards the land; they then slipped both anchors, and had just set the mainsail, when the vessel struck very heavily on the rocks with her starboard quarter and immediately went down in deep water; this was just about break of day, between 5 and 6 o'clock. Immediately after the vessel struck, the top-masts fell down, and went overboard, striking two of the crew in their fall and carrying the men overboard with them.

The Captain at once gave orders to get the boats out and to put the lady passengers into them; but as heavy seas were now breaking over the vessel, this could not be done. The Declarant with five others of the crew managed to get into the Lifeboat, which was at once washed overboard. When the Declarant came to himself he saw the boat drifting about, and at once swam to it, and held on until the boat drifted into a small bay or indentation close by where the ship struck. At daylight he found himself drifting towards the Beach, and letting go his hold of the boat, he swam ashore. By this time the Beach was strewn with cases and driftwood from the wreck.

> *As per Declaration* made by
> *Thomas R. Pearce*, Apprentice on board
> the late Ship "Loch Ard", and
> sole survivor of the Crew.

Captain Daish's conclusion was that the ship itself must be regarded as practically valueless. His statement reads:

Pursuant to instructions I proceeded to the scene of the wreck of the Ship "Loch Ard", about 15 miles west of Moonlight Head and near to the Sherbrook River.

On the Beach of a small cove I found a quantity of general Cargo washed up into a confused mass, some of it much broken. There were many broken cases and casks; also several iron tanks. I was shown a spar which seemed to be the mizen-topmast of the wreck; it was sticking up out of the water about 50 yards from the rocks of a small Island against which I was told the ship struck.

I went along the Coast to the eastward for a considerable distance but could see no sign of wreckage. On the following day I went to the westward and there I saw a number of Cases, Casks, and Bales; also deals and boards floating about in some of the gorges, this wreckage could only be got at by boats, as the Cliffs on this part of the Coast are nearly perpendicular.

There was nothing belonging to the ship of any value on the Beach, with the exception of a lifeboat, and this was badly shaken and injured.

The ship being sunk, in my opinion in about 60 feet of water, on such a wild and unprotected Coast I consider her of little value not more than £85 (eighty-five pounds) including the above mentioned life-boat.

I would therefore *Recommend* the immediate Sale by Public Auction for the benefit of all concerned.

(Signed) Joseph Daish.

Ten days after the wreck, salvage rights were sold by auction at the rooms of Lord and Hughes, Collins Street West, Melbourne. "It seemed as if the whole of the money making and speculative community of Melbourne were represented and taking part in the bidding. The first bid was £50. Then it went up in jumps of £50 until it reached £2000, amid great cheering. Gradually the price went up till the hammer fell at £2120 bid by Mr E. F. Howarth, who bought on behalf of a company at Geelong." The company referred to in this report, by the *Illustrated Australian News*, was Howarth, Miller and Matthews. Their setbacks will be mentioned later in this chapter.

The underwriters had to determine how the insurance covering the consigned goods and the proceeds of the salvage sale would be shared between the consignees in various states of Australia and as far away as New Zealand. All told there were 202 bills of lading. The invoice value of the goods was £68,456 (a considerably higher figure than shown on the ship's manifest, given at Appendix 5). Although the Melbourne sale had realized £2120, auction charges, agent's commission, salvage expenses, etc., had reduced this to a mere £1423/14/2. This and the insurance had to be apportioned between the 202 consignees in accordance with the value of each one's consignment. But numerous expenses had to be deducted. In the forty-seven page Salvage Statement* such claims as these appear:

For Hire of buggy to take Miss Carmichael from Coast to
Camperdown. Coach fare of do. £12.9/-
Charles McGillivray:
    For labour of 19 men employed at the wreck £32.4.9
    For services of self 5 days at wreck Loch Ard £7.10/-
Telegram to Aitken, Lilburn & Co. Glasgow "Loch Ard wrecked near Otway."
Hugh Gibson, Glenample Station. For Tarpaulin for men employed at

---

* Only one copy of this hand-written document, duplicated by lithograph, has so far been traced. In 1934 it was found in an old chest of drawers by a Sale (Vic.) second-hand dealer.

the wreck (now valueless) £6.5/-; 20 lb. Beef supplied for the men £5.10/-; Board of 2 men for 2 days £1.

Joseph Daish, Marine Surveyor. Proceeding from Melbourne to the wreck of the ship "Loch Ard", and Report. 7 days at £10.10/- per day. £73.10/-

When all expenses were met there was only sufficient money remaining from insurance and salvage for each consignee to receive 2.07716 per cent of the value of goods consigned to him. Six of the 202 cases are here quoted:

James McEwan & Co., consignments to value of £3338, recd. £69.6.8
John Danks   ,,   ,,   ,,   ,, £369 ,   ,,   £7.13.2
Paterson Laing & Co.   ,,   ,,   ,,   ,, £236 ,   ,,   £4.18/-
Michaelis Hallenstein & Co.   ,,   ,,   ,,   ,, £304 ,   ,,   £6.6.3
Allan & Co. (for three pianos in cases, valued at £104),   ,,   £2.3.3
Hugo Wertheim (for cases of sewing machines valued at £300), ,,   £6.4.7

To return to Messrs Howarth, Miller and Matthews. In the ten days between the wreck and the auction in Melbourne, Mr McGillivray and the Customs officers had hauled articles of value above high-water mark in the gorge. By 12th June it was estimated that £3000 worth of cargo had been recovered in this way. The barometer then began to fall and McGillivray urged that the recovered goods be moved farther from the sea. Unfortunately his advice was not taken and the bulk of the cargo was washed out in a violent storm.

Two days later Messrs Miller and Matthews reached the scene of the wreck. It was a dispiriting arrival. Only a small amount of cargo had been hauled by bullock team to the top of the gorge—spirits, chemicals, clothing and dress materials. The materials had been washed and were drying on improvised clotheslines. A rope ladder led down into the gorge. At the top a constable watched—not altogether successfully—for pilferers.

A load of goods salvaged in this way was sent off to Geelong: 68 cases of brandy, one cask of rum, 35 cases of candles, 10 cases of books, 55 boxes (contents unstated), and sundry cases of leather, drapery, carpets and soap. Sold at the Customs Shed on 12th July, they brought only £300. The wreckers had undoubtedly done much better.

Although this was a poor enough initial return, worse was to follow. Miller and Matthews had now to depend for success on cargo salvaged from the wreck itself. For this operation they chartered the ninety-ton paddle steamer *Napier* to survey the area. With divers aboard, the *Napier* set out from Port Campbell.

Although these divers had worked on a number of wrecks, they said later that none had lain "in so inaccessible a place as the unfortunate *Loch Ard*".

... The vessel was found to be lying broadside on to the bluff which she struck, in six fathoms of water. A portion of the wreck's stern is adrift and her fallen masts and sails and rigging form a regular network around her. Her upper decks are burst open, but there is a large quantity of heavy cargo which may be reclaimed: machinery, cases of galvanized iron; sheet copper, and in the lower hold a large quantity of railway iron.

Because the position was so exposed, the divers believed "an average of five working days a month is all that is likely to prevail for operations". Nevertheless they estimated that forty tons of merchandise a day could be recovered.

On the *Napier*'s third visit to the wreck, the weather suddenly changed for the worse, and in trying to get back into Port Campbell she was herself wrecked on the west side of the small harbour. There a few rusting remains of her may still be seen. Although the company hoped to replace her, their expenses proved so crippling that they were never able to return. In after years the daughter of the partner Miller stated that the only item of real value that had gone to her father was the porcelain peacock. Mr Miller and his diver, Thomas Keys, had found this bobbing undamaged in its case a few days after the storm and had had it hauled up the cliffs.

After the loss of the *Napier*, the *Loch Ard* was left undisturbed where she lay. As the years passed, the site of the wreck became a matter of local argument and speculation, and was to remain so for eighty-nine years.

28
THE INQUIRY

The *Argus* reporter, who appears to have delved into every aspect of the disaster, described Tom Pearce as "apparently none the worse for his narrow escape. He is as jolly and light-hearted as if he were still on the deck of the old ship, and, like most sailors, takes things as they come. . . ."

Pearce had lost everything in the wreck, including most of his clothing. On hearing this, the people of Warrnambool out-fitted him and presented him in addition with £100. He declined firmly to allow his photograph to be sold for his own benefit, asking instead that the proceeds go to a *Loch Ard* fund for those left by his shipmates.

The public were by now waiting avidly for every description of Pearce. Late in June they had an opportunity of seeing him in person when he went to Melbourne to attend the marine court of inquiry into the loss of his ship. This was held on 22nd June before members of the Steam Navigation Board at Melbourne Customs House. Pearce was the only witness. Captain Payne, who chaired the inquiry, was the Chief Harbourmaster of Melbourne. Other members of the board were Captain Fullarton, Captain Devlin, and Messrs Stephen and Sutherland. Even though much of the terminology of sail has become archaic, the *Argus* report of the inquiry is quoted almost in full because through it Pearce's character shines clearly:

Thomas Pearce, being sworn, said "I was an apprentice on board the *Loch Ard*. She was an iron vessel, her tonnage being 1623 tons, and she was owned by Messrs Aitken, Lilburn and Co. of Glasgow. We left

Gravesend about the 2nd or 3rd of March last. I was on board the ship all the time she was loading in the East India docks. Nothing particular transpired during the voyage, but I knew the compasses were a little out. We sighted one of the Cape de Verde Islands as we expected. We never saw Trinidad, or any portion of the coast of South America. It was the custom on board the *Loch Ard*, whenever an opportunity offered, to take azimuths in order to correct the compasses. I could not say whether amplitudes were taken. As we neared the Australian coast it was a matter of remark among the officers that there was a difference of three-quarters of a point between the standard compass and the binnacle compass. The standard compass was taken as the more correct one. This difference between the compasses was noticed fully a fortnight, if not more, before the ship was wrecked. I know of my own knowledge that every opportunity was seized for taking azimuths, but the weather for some time before the wreck had been rather thick and hazy. The last azimuth was taken the day before the wreck. From what I heard the officers say, the sights could not be depended upon. On Friday morning, May 31, we were steering N.E. by E., but after the meridian sights were obtained the course was altered to E. by N. or E.N.E., I am not quite sure which. That was the compass course, but I cannot say what the true course would be. I cannot say what the course was by the standard compass. On the afternoon before the wreck the second mate told me that we were 150 miles S.W. of Cape Otway. This was between 3 and 4 o'clock in the afternoon, when we were getting the anchors over the bows. I cannot say how far we were off the coast in a direct line, as I only asked what distance we were from Cape Otway. The wind was about S.W., as it was on our starboard quarter. The weather was fine, with a moderate breeze, and we were carrying all plain sail. Between 6 and 8 o'clock that evening the wind freshened, and at the same time hauled more to the southward, so that we had to brace the yards forward. About this time the captain gave orders to take in the three royals—the mizzen topgallant-sail, crossjack, and flying staysails. It was my first watch below, but I believe nothing particular occurred. When I came on deck again at midnight, we clewed up the topgallant-sails, backed the main yard, and got a cast of the lead. We got 63 fathoms. The lead was a patent one, and was armed. It showed a sandy bottom. A second cast was obtained, and this also gave 63 fathoms. We filled the main topsail again and to the best of my knowledge proceeded on the same course again. I was not on the poop at the time, and cannot therefore be quite certain on this point. After we filled on her the topgallant-sails were furled, and the foresail and mainsail hauled up, leaving the ship under the topsails, jib, and spanker. At

2 a.m. the captain gave orders to take in the upper fore and main topsails, haul down the inner jib, and brail in the spanker, leaving the ship under the three lower topsails and foretopmast staysail. I did not take any notice of the speed the ship was going through the water, as we were so busy shortening sail. At that time it was blowing pretty fresh, the wind being a little forward of the beam. We had not shortened sail on account of the wind, however, but because the captain knew we were approaching the land. It was expected that we should make the Cape Otway light about 3 o'clock on Saturday morning. Special orders had been given to the look-out man to keep a good look-out for both the land and the light, and during the middle watch a man was sent aloft about every quarter of an hour to see if he could make out the light. The lead was only hove at midnight, but I know that it was the intention of the captain to get another cast at 4 a.m. when the watch was relieved. It was at that time that the land was seen. There was a thick haze over the land, but it was clear overhead and to seaward. About 3 o'clock I noticed that the stars were shining brightly. It was just as the watch was being relieved at 4 o'clock that the land was seen. I think the captain and the man at the wheel saw it simultaneously. Our watch was going below—some had gone—when I heard the order to hoist up the stay-sails, and at the same time the captain ran forward, calling all hands on deck. We got the sail on her as quickly as possible by hoisting the main and mizzen topmast staysails, set the spanker, and hoisted the upper mizzen topsail. This was done with a view to bringing her round on the other tack, and as soon as she gathered way the captain gave the order, "All hands ready about." Every man was at that time on deck, but the upper fore and maintopsails were not hoisted, because there was not time to do so. When the helm was put hard down the ship just came up head to wind, and then commenced to fall off again, as there was not sail enough on her to bring her round. As soon as the captain saw she was beginning to fall off again, he ordered both anchors to be let go. The port anchor was let go first and was immediately followed by the star-board anchor. I should say we were then about half a mile from the shore, and I heard others estimate the distance the same. We were among the broken water. We did not range our cables in the *Loch Ard*, as we had a patent windlass, and the chain was payed out directly from the lockers. About 50 fathoms was given on each cable. We could soon see that the anchors were not holding, for every time the ship lifted with the sea she brought the anchors home. We gave her a little more cable, but could not give her much, as we were afraid of a rock astern to which we were very close. When the anchors were let go all the sails were clewed up. The anchors had, however, brought the ship head to

wind and sea, and the captain, finding that she was dragging, ordered the yards to be braced round on the port tack and the foretopmast staysail to be hoisted, keeping the sheet well to windward, so as to pay her head off. He then ordered the cables to be slipped and the topsails to be sheeted home, and while some of the men were slipping the cables, the rest of us were trying to get sail on her. We could not get the topsails sheeted home and therefore we got the port main tack down and hauled aft the sheet. As soon as her head began to fall off, the foretopmast staysail was hauled down, so that she should not fall off too much, but just as we got the main sheet aft the ship struck. At this time the mainsail was full, the wind being well abeam. We had no other sail on her, as there was no time. We were just about to hoist the mizzen topsail when she struck. Her starboard quarter appeared to strike a ledge of rock that was just awash. It was not far from the land and at every roll of the sea her yards would strike against the cliffs. The ship was just gathering way when she struck. I believe the rock made a great hole in her bottom, for she was bumping very heavily. The place against which she struck was not on the mainland, but on an island, about seventy yards distant, the cliffs of which are quite perpendicular. When the ship struck I heard the captain give orders to have the boats cleared away, and the port lifeboat made ready for the ladies. We had four boats on board, all of them being on the skids. The two boats on the forward skids were fitted in chocks, and were on their keels. These two boats were the gig and lifeboat. The davits were close to, and the falls were ready rove, but they were stopped up with rope yarns. The tackles were not hooked into the boats, but they were overhauled sufficiently to have been at once hooked on. The oars were in the boats. The lifeboat was fitted with enclosed air cases. I had heard that there were 16 or 18 cork life-belts on board, but I never saw them. Had the boats been hanging in the davits I have no doubt they could have been lowered into the water, but I do not think the passengers could have been got into them, owing to the heavy seas that were washing over the main deck. The seas were coming over both sides, as the back wash from the cliffs was bringing the sea in over the lee side. If the lifeboat had been lowered, I believe she would have been thrown in-board by the back wash from the cliffs. When the order was given to clear away the boats, I and five others went to the lifeboats. I do not know the names of all the others. I know there was Donahue, the engineer, and an able seaman named Smith. There were six of us in the boat. I cut the after gripe and kicked out the chock, while Smith cut the forward gripe, and just then a sea came on board and washed us all away. I did not see any of the passengers on deck at the time. I saw the captain on the poop. The seas were not so heavy on the poop as they were on the main deck. The ship seemed to me to be gradually sinking by the stern. I saw several of the seamen clinging to a portion of the upper maintopsail yard which had been broken by striking against the cliffs. The spars were falling in every direction, so much so that some of the sailors got into the cabin with the passengers in order to save themselves. I believe some ladies had put on cork jackets, and were going on deck, when they were at once washed away. When the sea struck the lifeboat and knocked it overboard it capsized, and I was underneath it. I never saw any of the others who were with me. I was under the boat for some time. The bottom boards had fallen down and were lying along the thwarts. That is where I kept. The boat floated very high, and there was plenty of air under her. I took out the plug so as to get more fresh air. I suppose I was under the boat about three quarters of an hour, but it seemed much more. The backwash, together with the ebb tide, must have taken the boat out to sea. When I came from under the boat I could see nothing of the ship, nothing but a lot of floating wreckage. I could not see anybody else floating. I went under the boat again, and the flood tide must then have drifted me in shore again, as the first thing I was aware of was the boat striking against a rock at the entrance of an inlet. This righted the boat, but as she was floating in I still kept to her; but when about half-way up the inlet she struck against the side of the cliffs and threw me out. I then struck out for the beach, which I reached, and found it covered with wreckage. The boat came on shore soon after I did. I cannot say how far I drifted out from the land during the time I was under the boat. I think the ship must have gone down stern first, and with her mainsail set, as when I was washed overboard she was slowly going down. When I got on shore I looked for some place to get shelter from the wind and found a cave. After being there for some time, I should say about an hour, and having a good rest, I went to look among the wreckage for something to eat. I then heard someone calling out and at first thought that it was somebody on the cliffs above me, but I could not see anybody. I heard a second cry, and then looked out to sea and saw a lady clinging to a spar. I saw it was one of the passengers, but could not tell who it was at first. I afterwards found that it was Miss Eva Carmichael. I swam out to her and brought her on shore and then managed to get her into the cave. The spar to which she was clinging had struck against the same point of rock as the boat did when I was thrown out. We afterwards received assistance from Mr Gibson, a squatter residing in the neighbourhood. The particulars that have appeared in the press relative to subsequent matters are quite correct. We had fine weather during our passage from the Cape, but with occasional gales. The ship was stiff and sailed well on a wind. We have got as much as 14 knots an hour out of her. Coming from the Cape we were mostly on the port tack. The ship had not been braced up so sharp on the starboard tack as she was on the night of the wreck. On that night she heeled over about 5 deg., increasing to 10 deg. towards 4 o'clock on the Saturday morning. The course was altered on Friday, after the meridian sights were taken. I did not hear that the soundings we took at midnight brought us nearer the land than was expected. Among the cargo was a great quantity of railway iron, machinery, and sheet iron. The railway iron was stowed in the main hold, and the sheet iron was stowed aft of that. It was stowed on its flat, and not on its edge. Above that was stowed the miscellaneous cargo. There was a great deal of beer, wines, and spirits on board, most of which was stowed in the after hold. I have been three voyages in the *Loch Ard.* There has been no alteration in the position of the compasses since I have been in her, but they had been adjusted by swinging the ship before she started on each voyage. I have never known them to be taken on shore to have the needles remagnetized. I have heard Captain Buchanan, a former captain of the ship, say that the compasses were bad, and that he had never been with worse ones. I am not aware that the compasses were ever adjusted in order to ascertain their heeling error."

Captain Payne said, "The Board must congratulate you, Mr. Pearce, on the clear and distinct statement you have made, not only respecting the wreck itself but of the occurrences previous to it. It is evident you have had your wits about you, and have taken notice of what has been going on in the ship, or you could not have made such a clear statement as you have done. I congratulate you, and wish you every success."

Mr. Pearce—"Thank you, sir."

The proceedings then terminated.

Pearce's statement was sent on to the British Board of Trade. Soon after receiving it they awarded him their silver medal for gallantry.

29
WEEKS AT
GLENAMPLE

Life for the Gibsons remained greatly disrupted. To give Eva companionship and to provide help with the many additional tasks of the house, Mrs Gibson asked a nineteen-year-old Princetown girl, Jane Shields, sister of William who had assisted with the rescue, to stay with them. Perhaps common links with Ireland drew the two together. Hour after hour Jane would sit brushing the bereaved girl's waist-long hair, which for days after the wreck remained matted and tangled.

An extraordinary succession of Carmichael belongings was washed ashore in the days following the wreck. First Eva's writing desk, in which were photographs of her parents; then, on the day of the burials, "there was picked up on the beach a circular india-rubber air cushion. Upon examination it was found to have a piece cut out of the outer edge, and inside of it were found two of Dr Carmichael's medical diplomas and a Masonic certificate or degree." Miss Carmichael, the *Argus* continued, "is unable to explain how the papers came inside the cushion, but as it was always on Dr Carmichael's bed in perfect state, she supposes that either he or her mamma must at the last moment have cut the hole in the cushion and put the papers in it, trusting to their getting ashore safely, or probably thinking that the ship would not go down, and that the india-rubber cushion would keep the papers dry".

The same *Argus* described Eva as a girl "of strong constitution and intensely buoyant spirits". The buoyant spirits puzzled many people. Hugh Gibson, in his letter to his stepmother, went on to describe Eva:

Although only nineteen years of age [she] is fully 5 feet 8 inches high [two and a half inches taller than Tom Pearce] and 12 stone weight, pale complexion, not to say pretty, but good looking and sometimes very fascinating—I don't think she knows yet the loss that she has suffered. Her spirits are good; in fact had it not been for her lively disposition she would not have recovered. Some people are surprised that they do not find her downcast, but it just amounts to this: that had she been broken she would not be living now for anyone to see.

She is bent on going home to Ireland and as soon as I get answers to some correspondence which I have instituted on her behalf, she may leave before long. Lavinia will most likely go with her—she must— Symonette has given us an invitation to Hammerdale which I have reason to believe will be only too gladly accepted. [Hammerdale was the St Kilda home of the Gemmell family, friends of the Gibsons.]

Hugh Gibson continued his letter on 6th July:

Tonight I have letters which have determined us to start Miss Carmichael for Melbourne on or about Wednesday next, the 10th inst.

You perhaps would like to know something more of Miss C. and what I now tell you is in strict confidence. We cannot make her out exactly. She is a puzzle to all who have seen her. She can talk of her Papa and Mama and Raby and her brothers and sisters and tell what they did and said and laugh; still she must feel it though she does not show it. Just imagine her being here and hearing of bodies floating about and knowing that they might be those of her family and still not show any sign. The thought is something dreadful.

At the first, as Anna said in a letter to Lavinia, it would appear as if we had a daughter thrown from the sea to us, but I soon put that notion to the one side. To wind up I may state that both Lavinia and I take a tremendous interest in her and now it is my main thought how to get her fairly off in good hands for old Ireland. She is Irish to the backbone.

We have letters from the Chief Secretary etc. We did nothing else than we could have helped.

I fancy Lavinia has been rather remiss in answering Anna's, so this might do for her as well.

It would seem probable that Anna and Lavinia were sisters. The letter closes with the rather stiff formality of the era: "I am your affectionate son, Hugh H. Gibson." The letter he had received from the Chief Secretary read:

I feel it would be unbecoming were I to allow to pass without some public acknowledgement the humanity and benevolence you evinced on the occurrence of the shipwreck of the *Loch Ard*, or fail to express the admiration the Government feels of your exertions to save the lives of the persons belonging to that unfortunate vessel. The kindness and devotion shown by Mrs Gibson and yourself towards the two young persons who were rescued through your instrumentality have deeply affected all in Australia, and left an impression in their minds which no lapse of time can efface.

I am aware that you must have been subjected to considerable and unavoidable expense in maintaining the numerous persons who visited the scene of the wreck for public or private purposes since the catastrophe occurred, as well as by the derangement of your ordinary business caused by the unusual presence of so many visitors. I need only say it will afford great pleasure to the Government to reimburse you for any losses that you may have incurred, if you will be so good as to state their amount.

I have the honour to be, Sir, your most obedient servant,

GRAHAM BERRY

There is no evidence to suggest that Hugh Gibson accepted reimbursement, but he did accept from the local people a specially inscribed buggy; one that had gained first prize at the Geelong show for the carriage-maker Augustus Grote. It was presented by Peter McArthur and was used at Glenample for the remainder of Gibson's years there.

A fortnight after receipt of the Chief Secretary's letter, Hugh Gibson heard from the Governor of Victoria:

MY DEAR SIR,

The Chief Secretary (Mr Berry) has already conveyed to you the warm thanks of the Victorian Government for your noble exertions at the period of the wreck of the *Loch Ard* and for the kind and generous hospitality which Mrs Gibson and you showed to the survivors. I desire to add the expression of my own deep sense of your admirable conduct.

Lady Bowen and I will be very glad to see Mrs Gibson and yourself and Miss Carmichael at the Government House, if you will call on us on your next visit to Melbourne.

I trust that Miss Carmichael's health has not been impaired by all that she has suffered. I have had great pleasure in meeting young Mr Pearce, whose modesty equals his merit.

Lady Bowen unites with me in compliments and best wishes to yourself and Mrs Gibson and Miss Carmichael.

> I remain, my dear Sir,
> Yours very faithfully,
> G. N. BOWEN

A week after this letter was received, Eva Carmichael was ready to leave Glenample. In his account written many years later Hugh Gibson said:

She gave us to understand from the first that she wished to return to Ireland. I had numerous applications from people wishing to receive her, and it often took me a good deal of time sitting up at night answering the letters. Theatrical people, and others wanted to get her, but I turned a deaf ear to all of them, feeling that in her state she would spoil herself.

To lose father, mother, sisters and brothers would try anyone, and we thought that she was a little off her head. At the end of July we determined to make a start. [Actually they started during the second week of July.] First a few days at Mr McArthur's Meningoort, then from Camperdown to Colac by coach where we got the train to Geelong and Melbourne. . . . On our way down, the platforms at Colac and Geelong were crowded by people wishing to get a sight of her, and at Geelong the crowd was so great, that to get the ladies out of the carriage for a few minutes a ruse had to be resorted to. I had an acquaintance in another carriage, and he, seeing how matters stood, came to the rescue by giving out that some *other* ladies in another carriage were the objects of interest. The people then congregated there, and left our carriage free.

But a *Geelong Advertiser* reporter managed to speak to Eva. "Police had to protect Miss Carmichael when she moved to the refreshment room. She wore a black silk dress and a grey waterproof ulster; black hat with full veil. She said she wanted to return to her former home in Ireland as soon as possible, but on a steamer and not a sailing ship."

Tom Pearce was among those waiting at Geelong to meet her. The reporter saw him as a "short stout thickset young fellow but not strikingly prepossessing in appearance. He is of quiet demeanor, and apparently he does not court anything like praise or demonstration. The young ladies were particularly desirous of shaking hands with the *Loch Ard* hero. He gave brief and bashful answers to the numerous questions put to him."

Much to his own discomfort, Tom was now a national figure. A poem was addressed to him by a poet no longer identifiable: "To the Hero of the *Loch Ard*". It appeared in a little publication, *Australian Verse Drift*. Certainly it expressed the drift of the public's feelings and wishes.

Where the sunken rocks defy,
And the dead enshrouded lie
    As ocean guests,
Where the waves in mountains rise,
And the dark clouds hide the skies,
    The *Loch Ard* rests.

Where the rude and rugged walls
Catch the snow-white spray that falls
    As bridal veils,
Where the breakers ceaseless roar,
And the foaming billows pour,
    And tempest wails,

There old Neptune's gallant son,
Fearless fought with death, and won
    Fair Evaline;
From the deep he heard her cry,
Bravely for her dared to die
    Unsung, unseen.

Battled with the curling deep,
Where the fierce winds angry sweep
    O'er coral graves;
Nobly bore her to the beach,
Laid her safe beyond the reach
    Of angry waves.

Scal'd the high and rocky steeps
Where the lonely eagle sleeps,
    The feather'd chief;
Found the shepherd's winding track,
Brought the welcome tidings back,
    And staid his grief.

Let the Victor's praise be sung,
Let a fadeless wreath be hung
   Around his name.
Hero of the lost *Loch Ard*,
Take thy merited reward,
   Immortal fame.

30
"THE FEELING OF
THOUSANDS—"

Although the court of inquiry was unable to determine what had caused the *Loch Ard* to be off course, the press coverage brought Tom Pearce oppressive attention. A Melbourne man recalled passing him at this time while walking with a friend in Collins Street. Pearce, on hearing the two mention his name, cast them a "beseeching glance to be left alone".

In the same week as the inquiry, the Governor of Victoria presented him with a gold watch, chain and locket in the presence of numerous dignitaries. The watch bore the inscription: "Presented to Thomas Pearce by the Government of Victoria, for his noble conduct in risking his own life to save that of a fellow-passenger after his providential escape on the occasion of the wreck of the *Loch Ard*, near Sherbrooke River, on the coast of this colony, on 1st June, 1878." Receiving the watch, Pearce simply said, "I thank Your Excellency for the honour you have done me, and hope I shall always do my duty towards my country."

On 20th June, in Melbourne Town Hall, he was awarded the gold medal of the Humane Society. According to the *Spectator*:

The announcement that Pearce would be present caused so much excitement, that long before the hour for opening the doors, the neighbourhood of the building was thronged with eager seekers for admission. When the proceedings commenced, it is said over five thousand persons had gained entrance to the great hall, and as soon as the "observed of all observers" appeared on the platform, the enthusiasm of the spectators found relief in cheering which lasted five minutes. He acknowledged the ovation with a modest bow, and took his seat on the left hand of Sir Redmond Barry; and when the latter, having handed the first gold medal of the society to Pearce, shook him heartily by the hand, there was another great outburst of applause.

No doubt Pearce hoped that this would be the end of the adulation, but further gatherings, in both Melbourne and Sydney, became extravaganzas of public acclaim.

In Sydney, on 27th July, "seven thousand persons (a large proportion of whom were ladies) assembled at the Exhibition Building to welcome the gallant midshipman". There Pearce suffered a presentation of nautical instruments and a homily from the Lady Mayoress. "Mr Pearce thanked the Mayoress for her kindness . . . and bowed his acknowledgement to the assemblage, which cheered vociferously."

Only three days later he was required to attend a testimonial concert in the Melbourne Town Hall. The *Argus* announcement made it sound a gala occasion:

TONIGHT   TONIGHT   TONIGHT

TONIGHT   TONIGHT   TONIGHT

Orchestral Concert
In aid of the
PEARCE TESTIMONIAL FUND
And for the
Distressed Sufferers
Of the
LOCH ARD
Under the distinguished patronage and in
the presence of
His Excellency the Governor
and Lady Bowen
Her Majesty's Ministers
The Right Worshipful the Mayor and Corporation of
the City of Melbourne
Her Majesty's Naval Service
and the
Merchant Service
Musical Director, Mr David Lee
The following artists have kindly volunteered their
gratuitous services . . .

The names of twenty artists followed, plus a "Grand Orchestra of 50 Performers". The prospective audience was warned that "in consequence of the enormous length of the programme NO ENCORES whatever can possibly be acceded to".

Many Melburnians had hoped that Eva Carmichael, too, would attend the concert, but, not surprisingly, she declined to do so. When Pearce arrived with the Governor every seat was filled and over a hundred people were standing. The organizers had included in the concert programme a number of melancholy songs presumably regarded as appropriate for the occasion. "Launch the Lifeboat" was sung and "Out of the Rocks" and "O My Lost Love".

Pearce survived the concert as splendidly as he had survived the wreck and the presentations. The Victorian Government awarded him a sum of £1000; a schottische was composed in his honour. But there was one wish of the public that seems to have embarrassed him more than all else: they wanted nothing less than his marriage to Eva Carmichael; or, if that could not be granted them, then the knowledge that a humble sailor was suffering unrequited love after being rejected by a young lady of higher station. A Rev. Thomas Jones "gave expression to the feeling of thousands when he said, 'All he wanted now was to see them married to each other' ", as if their experience were a guarantee of happiness ever after.

But there was no marriage; no clear news of a rejection; no *Pinafore* discovery that Tom Pearce was of equal station. (To a degree this came later.) In fact the brief association of the two young people was nearing its end. To the Australian public their story was to end in anti-climax.

Understandably Eva Carmichael wished to return home as soon as the steamship booking could be made, but she was entirely without money. Hugh Gibson "thought it the duty of the Government, under the circumstances, to undertake the risk of outlay. I eventually got the Premier to advance £200 as a loan, which covered all expenses of passage, besides putting a few pounds in her pocket for the way."

Nearly three months after losing her family Eva Carmichael was farewelled from Port Melbourne on the P. & O. steamer

Tanjore. Tom Pearce was among those who saw her off, whether with sorrow or relief one can only conjecture.

About a year after the girl's arrival home she sent Hugh Gibson a bank draft for £200 in repayment of the government loan. But Gibson had other ideas. Among the Carmichael documents to drift ashore there had been a letter from the son in Australia "which showed me clearly," said Gibson, "how the family stood for wealth. This letter I showed only to Mr McArthur and Mr Gemmell, and destroyed it." On the basis of the letter he persuaded the Government to allow him to return Eva's money to her.

One might infer from this that the family stood badly for wealth. Other evidence suggests that this was by no means the case, that sufficient remained for Eva to be left in comfort. Among the Carmichael papers washed ashore was one mentioned in the *Leader*, but not by Gibson. This was a draft on the Union Bank for £4000. There was also later evidence, from Eva's own son, that Dr Carmichael had not been dependent upon his medical practice, but derived income from church tithes in Ireland.

During 1879 the wayward William Carmichael, the only surviving son of the family, came to Melbourne as chief officer of the *Loch Ness*. He went by train to Colac, then by coach to Port Campbell over rough roads with "a driver who pulled aside for nothing smaller than a barrel, on a road only visible to a blacktracker". He had a tall headstone erected over the Carmichael grave to the memory of the lost members of his family and to record his sister's rescue:

> *"Shall Not the Judge of all the Earth do Right"*
> *Sacred*
> *to*
> *the Memory of*
> *Mrs Evory Carmichael*
> *and*
> *Miss Raby Carmichael*
> *Whose Bodies lie Beneath*
> *Also*
> *In Remembrance of*

Dr Evory Carmichael
Misses Margaret and Annie
Charmichael
Masters Evory and Thomas Carmichael
All of Whom were Lost in the Calamitous Wreck
of the "Loch Ard"
Saturday, June 1st, 1878
This Stone is Erected by
Eva and William Carmichael,
The Former of Whom
Was most Miraculously Preserved,
In Affectionate Remembrance of Their Deceased
Parents, Brothers and Sisters

Near by a second stone was later erected:

In Memory
of
Arthur Mitchell
and Reginald Jones
Who Lost Their Lives
In the Wreck
of the Loch Ard
1st June 1878

31
PEARCE'S LATER YEARS

If ever a man deserved a long and happy life it was Tom Pearce. As it happened, he and his sons were dogged by tragedy at sea. After being lionized in Australia, Pearce returned to the Loch Line, joining the *Loch Sunart* for a further voyage to England. This was the last three-masted ship to be built for the Loch Line. Launched in 1878, she must have had the shortest life of any of them. Pearce's voyage in her was her last. She was wrecked on the Skulmartin Rock off the coast of Ireland on 11th January 1879. Again Pearce reached shore alive.

In Australia rumours spread that he had been taken to the nearest house, which happened to be that of Eva Carmichael; that she had nursed him back to health and that they had married. The wide circulation of this story shows that it reflected the hopes of many thousands of Australians. Years afterwards, in 1921, it was even repeated in Basil Lubbock's *Colonial Clippers*. There was no substance to it.

In January 1883 Pearce transferred permanently to steamships, joining the Royal Mail Steam Packet Company—the present Royal Mail Lines. At that time he had his last contact with Eva Carmichael. This is mentioned in a letter from Miss Carmichael to the curator of the Warrnambool Museum. The curator had written asking Miss Carmichael if she would write an account of her escape from the wreck of the *Loch Ard* so that it could be kept for the people of the district. Her reply was written from Montpellier Villa, Cheltenham, England, on 21st January 1884:

I am afraid I cannot write a narrative about the wreck, as I never have written a story of any sort, but I shall try and if I think my sad story is not well enough written for such a place of interest, as I am sure your museum is, you will forgive my not sending it.

Although I am so many miles away from Australia my thoughts are almost always there, not only my sad thoughts about those that I loved and lost there, but my brightest thoughts that take me back to Glenample with all the sympathy and affection of my dear friends Mrs and Mr Gibson and then the other dear friends at whose houses I stayed, many of whom are "gone to be with Christ which is far better" and then I think of the real and true kindness of all Australians to me, the letters from many and the kind consideration of all.

There was a postscript: "You will be glad to hear that Tom Pearce is on board the H.M.S. [*sic*] *Solent*. I heard from him last month. He wrote from the West Indies and seemed in good spirits. I have not seen him since we parted at Melbourne. I believe he is to be married next year or perhaps this, but I do not know the young lady."

A sensitive letter, yet one feels it was less than generous to relegate Pearce to a postscript. Perhaps it would have been regarded as unseemly in that era for Eva Carmichael to have mentioned him with any show of warmth or even of gratitude, especially as he was about to marry. His fiancée was the sister of his fellow apprentice on the *Loch Ard*, Robert Strasenbergh, who had been his closest friend.

On 25th March 1898, at the age of thirty-eight, Pearce was given his first command, the *Larne*. He was to remain a master with the Royal Mail for the remaining nine years of his career.

In 1905 and 1906 the sea dealt him two further blows, from which he was never to recover. He had two sons, both of whom went to sea. The elder, T. R. Pearce, joined the Loch Line at the age of fifteen, just as his father had done. In 1905 he made his first voyage in the *Loch Vennachar*.

Bound from Glasgow to Adelaide, [says Basil Lubbock] she came on the overdue list. . . . On 29th September, the ketch *Annie Witt* arrived at Adelaide, and her captain reported picking up a reel of blue printing paper 18 miles N.W. of Kangaroo Island. This paper was identified as part of the *Loch Vennachar*'s cargo. A search was made on Kangaroo

Island and wreckage was discovered which made the disaster only too sure. . . . As if the fatal curse of Jonah had been transmitted from father to son, T. R. Pearce, a son of the twice wrecked Tom Pearce, was one of the apprentices lost in her. [Tom, in fact, had been three times wrecked.]

The *Loch Vennachar* had run onto Young Rocks.

In 1906 Pearce senior suffered his second blow. He had taken command that year of the 4572-ton *Orinoco*. On his second voyage in her, in a thick fog on the approaches to Cherbourg, she collided with the 14,000-ton German steamer *Kaiser Wilhelm der Grosse*. The clipper bows of the *Orinoco* penetrated the side of the German vessel well above the waterline, killing four passengers. The *Orinoco* launched a lifeboat, but three men manning it lost their lives.

Pearce was cleared of all blame, but he seems to have declined rapidly in health after this time. A year later, on 4th November 1907, he was seized with a fit, said to have been caused by the improbable-sounding combination of a kidney condition and a gangrenous toe. Following this he was granted three months' leave from the company. His position was held for him, but he was never able to resume duty. He died on 15th December 1908, aged forty-nine.

A brief obituary appeared in the *Argus* of 22nd January 1909:

A private cable message has been received in Melbourne announcing the death in Ireland of Captain Tom Pearce, the hero of the wreck of the *Loch Ard* at Peterborough in 1879 [*sic*]. Pearce, who was an apprentice on board the vessel, displayed signal gallantry in rescuing Miss Carmichael, the only passenger who was not drowned. At the time of his death, which occurred on December 15th, he was in the service of the Royal Mail Steam Packet Company.

Years later the silver medal for gallantry awarded Pearce by the Board of Trade was discovered in a Sydney junk shop by an antique dealer.

Pearce was survived by his younger son, Robert Strasenbergh Pearce. Although the "curse of Jonah" was to continue, the story of this second son is related in some detail for it depicts a man worthy of his father. In the First World War Robert Pearce was awarded the Distinguished Service Cross while in command of a mine-sweeper. He survived and returned to the merchant service, eventually to the Australia and New Zealand run with Shaw Savill. In 1938 he joined the 12,843 ton motor ship *Waimarama* as first officer while the ship was still under construction. The Shaw Savill Line's official Second World War History relates that: "He was appointed temporarily to her command in Melbourne in 1941, but he made such an excellent impression on the voyage home that he was retained in the post in spite of the fact that he was one of the most junior commanders in the Company." His home was now in Sydney.

On August 13th 1942 the *Waimarama* was one of fourteen ships in a convoy bound for the relief of Malta; she was carrying high octane aviation fuel. The convoy came under devastating attack and only four of the fourteen reached their destination. The log of one of these, the *Melbourne Star*, records the *Waimarama*'s end:

0815 Dive Bomber and Torpedo attack.
0816 *Wairmarama*. Hit by full stick of 4 1000 pound bombs, catching fire and exploding, sunk in 2 minutes .... Smoke rose to 10,000 feet.... Debris rained upon us.

Of a crew of 128, only 11 survived. Robert Strasenbergh Pearce, then aged fifty-three, was among those lost.

32
EVA TOWNSHEND

And Eva Carmichael—what later became of her? What manner of woman did she prove to be?

Quite apart from question of "station", even the most romantically inclined could hardly have expected her to have been happy as the wife of a man as committed to the sea as Pearce was. In 1884, the year that she wrote to the curator of the Warrnambool Museum, she married Thomas Achilles Townshend, C.E., of County Cork, a man fifteen years her senior. His place of birth was Castle Garrycloyne near Blarney.

It is doubtful that she ever completed a story for the Warrnambool Museum. The wreck was not a happening one could expect her to reconstruct with anything other than distress of mind.

After her marriage Eva Townshend lived with her husband in Bedford. She corresponded still with the Gibsons. In 1906 Hugh Gibson recorded in his reminiscences: "She says that until she left Australia she never realized the kindness shown to her by the Australians and till this day she still harps on that theme. She is now Mrs Townshend, mother of three sons, the eldest 21 years of age is a Lieutenant in the 1st Bedfordshire Regiment and in India, the other two are also qualifying for the Army." Again Gibson recalls her fearful experience in the wreck: "Her vitality must have been great. [She] only had a small spar—a boat's mast—to take her and must have been several hours in the sea in the dead of winter. . . . With her holding onto the spar were two strong young men and they both succumbed."

In 1934, when she was seventy-six, her attention was drawn to Basil Lubbock's version of her supposed marriage to Pearce. This led her to trace the one member of the Pearce family then still living, Robert Pearce. Whether her motive sprang from emotions stirred up on hearing again of the *Loch Ard*, or a feeling of regret for not having written previously, or from a wish to correct any misunderstanding about her links with Pearce, cannot be altogether determined from her letter to the son. Overtones of all three motives are detectable.

Robert Pearce was at that time chief officer of the *Pukeha* on the New Zealand run. Having traced him, Eva Townshend wrote her letter, but for several months it followed him around the world:

You will perhaps understand my writing to you when I tell you that I was the Miss Carmichael wrecked in the *Loch Ard* with your father. When we were found, starving, we went our separate ways without establishing a connecting link for further communication. . . . Last week someone brought us a book by Basil Lubbock called *Colonial Clippers* in which the tragedy of the *Loch Ard* is dealt with. The writer suggests that I nursed your father back to health a year later when he was wrecked on the *Loch Sunart* and that we eventually married and lived happily ever after, like the old story books have it. Unfortunately I never set eyes on your father after the *Loch Ard* wreck and only by accident at this distant date did I learn of your existence. . . . Many years back I married and settled in Bedford. . . . But now that I know where you are, and who you are, if an old woman in her seventies can be found time for a chat over those tragic days, I will be pleased to hear from you on your return from Australia. I have never forgotten that I owe my life to your father.

A week after she wrote this letter, Eva Townshend's life ended. When he discovered this some months later, Robert Pearce sent the letter to the London *Star*. It was published by that paper and republished in Australia. The Melbourne *Sun* of 18th July 1935 made a mild sensation of it: DEATH CHEATS WOMAN AFTER FIFTY-SEVEN YEAR QUEST. FOUND SON OF RESCUER, BUT DIED AFTER POSTING LETTER.

No evidence suggests that Eva Carmichael sought Tom

Pearce's whereabouts for fifty-seven years, or even for the twenty-five years between his *Solent* letter to her and his death. He was based in England during his seafaring life, and his movements, as a ship's officer, are not difficult to trace even today.

Of Eva Townshend's three sons, one, Lieutenant-Colonel R. S. H. Townshend, was alive in 1962. In that year, at the age of seventy-five, he replied to inquiries made of him by Mr Alasdair Loch of Sydney, a keen student of the *Loch Ard* story. In his letter to Mr Loch, Lieutenant-Colonel Townshend related that after the wreck of the *Loch Ard* his mother "received many proposals of marriage, perhaps a dozen, including one from Tom Pearce. Tom Pearce was, I think, an apprentice. She spoke of him sometimes as a 'cabin boy'. From his photograph he was a fine handsome young man. The reason she declined his offer of marriage was largely the fruit of class distinction, I think, class prejudice being very strong in Ireland in those days."

Had Pearce in fact asked the girl to marry him, or was this a fanciful story handed down years later from mother to son? Or again, in the terms of those days, had the girl been "compromised" by circumstances—had Pearce believed it a point of honour that he should propose to her because people might make suppositions about his hours alone with her? It appears that this might well have been the case.

Mrs Marjorie Moseley, a South Australian, had often been told the story of the wreck as a child and had as often asked her mother why Eva and Tom had not married. In 1924, while visiting the South of France, she met "an elderly, well set-up woman" who proved to be the ageing Eva Townshend. She was there to tend her husband's grave, he having died two years before in Monte Carlo. "Out came my old query, 'Why didn't you marry Tom Pearce?' She sat down on a chair as if shocked and said, 'I haven't been asked that for fifty years.' . . . She mentioned that Tom had asked her to marry him as in those days she had been compromised by their time together, but she had hardly ever noticed him on the ship and he had a lass in Scotland."

People around Glenample had observed that, rather than exhibiting fondness for her, Pearce had in fact been embarrassed when Eva had impulsively thrown her arms around him and called him her "saviour".

If Pearce did indeed propose and if it was class distinction that led Eva Carmichael to decline, an odd twist is given this by a report which appeared soon after the wreck in a relatively obscure newspaper, the *Kilmore Free Press*.

Now that the papers throughout the colony are teeming with accounts of the total wreck of the *Loch Ard*, and the heroic conduct of Tom Pearce in rescuing Eva Carmichael, it may be interesting to supply a link with reference to the history of the young gentleman named which we have noticed wanting. In the first place then we are in a position to state that the name of the surviving hero of the *Loch Ard* is not Tom Pearce but Tom Millet the son of the late Richard Millet, C.E., who was engaged in effecting land surveys in this district under the Land Act, 1862, about fifteen years ago, and grandson of the late Thomas Millet Esq., proprietor of an estate called Millbrook, near Cappawhite, county Tipperary, Ireland, where the gallant rescuer of Miss Carmichael was also born, having been brought to the colony when about three or four years of age. Soon after Mr Richard Millet concluded his professional duties here, he proceeded to New Zealand, leaving behind him in one of the Melbourne suburbs a wife and family, including the hero Tom, now called Pearce. Mr Millet had not been long in New Zealand when he took ill and died and his widow soon after married Captain Pearce, commander of the ill-fated *Gothenburg*. The step-children of the latter, including Tom, evidently adopted the name of Pearce, whilst the real name was that we have stated, a name honoured and held in high esteem where it was best known.

Assuming the *Kilmore Free Press* to be correct, the social gap between Eva Carmichael and Tom Millet was not as great as was first believed; nevertheless, it would not have been sufficiently narrow to have met the dictates of Eva's Victorian snobbishness.

It is difficult after a lapse of so many years to determine what manner of girl Eva Carmichael was. A family friend who was a contemporary of her eldest son has recorded an impression of her in her later years, when her three sons were mature men, as "a strong-minded, determined woman—she made all her three sons go into the Army". Eva herself had told I. Keith McIntyre of her Plantagenet antecedents. "She spoke," he said, "with the naturalness and rich accent of those maidens of the higher class." We can sense his upward glance. Then his eyes are turned down to the lesser mortal: Pearce "is unassuming, civil and tolerably well educated".

Snobbery apart, one is left with the impression that Eva was one of those indomitable women of Victorian times—proud, strict, prudish, unflinching, they expected obedience from their children and no whimpering. No submissive spirit could have clung to a spar for five hours in a winter sea. We could wish that she had not let her rescuer slip so far out of her life.

In 1932 the death occurred in Victoria of Jane Osborne (*née* Shields), the Princetown girl whose companionship had helped Eva Carmichael back to health. As she herself had wished, she was buried near the Carmichael grave above the Loch Ard Gorge. A dinner set given her by Eva is cherished still by her family.

Eva Townshend's own death notice appeared in the Melbourne *Argus* on 16th May 1934: "Townshend—On 8th April, at her residence, Bedford, England, Evaline Victoria, widow of the late Thomas Achilles Townshend, C.E., of Co. Cork, Ireland, in her 74th year. Mrs Townshend was the Eva Carmichael who, with the late Tom Pearce, were the only two survivors of the ship *Loch Ard*, which was wrecked near Port Campbell on June 1st 1878."

33
A HYPOTHESIS

As a competent board of inquiry was unable to determine in 1878 why Captain Gibb was off course, it is perhaps presumptuous for a layman, looking over scanty evidence many years later, to offer a conclusion. Nevertheless, there are a few shreds of evidence that warrant a hypothesis.

No copy of the official transcript of evidence having so far been located, it has only been possible to work from the *Argus* account of the proceedings quoted in Chapter 28. This has every appearance of being a verbatim report, but as such it does not incorporate the conclusions that the board undoubtedly recorded after Pearce's evidence had been heard.

The *Loch Ard*'s chronometer does not appear to have been the cause of the wreck; Gibb was about as far west of Otway as he reckoned himself to be on the evening of 31st May. But it might have struck readers interested in navigation that there is a significant contradiction between two pieces of information given by Pearce to the board. Pearce stated that the second mate had told him on the afternoon before the wreck that they were "150 miles S.W. of Cape Otway". This would have placed the ship well south of the usual approach to Bass Strait. It seems doubtful that the board could have plotted this Otway bearing and distance. Had they done so, it would have been immediately evident to them that it placed the *Loch Ard* in the latitude of the north-west tip of Tasmania, or twenty-seven miles farther south than the most southerly tip of King Island. Yet Gibb had altered course to starboard, to all appearances moving farther south of his proper route.

The most obvious reason for a navigator deciding to alter course to starboard when approaching the western entrance to Bass Strait is to avoid Cape Otway. If this is what Gibb did, it strongly suggests that he did not himself believe the ship to be south of the normal route, but north of it. In this he was correct.

The scrap of evidence from the second mate is, of course, open to doubt—Pearce might well have misheard him—but when all the circumstances are examined there is every reason to believe that the noon sights did indeed show the *Loch Ard* to be south of the normal route.

Eva Carmichael told the *Argus* reporter that the Chief Officer had taken and worked out the noon sun sights that day. She and her sister Raby had done so as well. All their results agreed, but the sights were poor.

It seems likely that the sights were poor because of haze on the landward horizon. The haze later thickened, it will be remembered, and obscured the coast.

Haze on the horizon would give an uncertain datum from which to measure the meridian altitude of the sun. Gibb would have been aware that the angle between the apparent horizon and the sun would be less than that measured from the obscured true horizon. The smaller angle obtained would give a latitude farther south than was actually the case. How much farther south Gibb could not with certainty tell. He could only know that he was considerably closer to the coast than the noon sight indicated. Common sense dictated an alteration of course away from the mainland; the very haze itself was indicative of land—there was none to seaward. In determining the extent of the alteration, of course, he had to back his judgement.

It might be said that Gibb accepted a degree of risk, that he ought to have anchored and waited for the haze to disperse; indeed, the *Illustrated Sydney News* did say this. But then Gibb was expected to exercise judgement after weighing up the probabilities of a situation. This he must have done on innumerable occasions previously. A master dependent upon sextant and chronometer, compass, log and lead, and with a company demanding fast passages of him, could not always be perfectly sure before making a decision.

He was right in altering course by a considerable amount to starboard. As it eventuated, the alteration should have been at least five degrees more, or made earlier. Circumstances were much against him. Even then, his seamanship during the *Loch Ard*'s last manoeuvres came close to snatching victory.

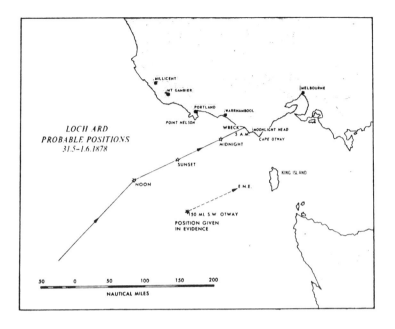

LOCH ARD
PROBABLE POSITIONS
31.5–1.6.1878

MILLICENT
MT GAMBIER
PORTLAND
POINT NELSON
WARRNAMBOOL
WRECK
MOONLIGHT HEAD
CAPE OTWAY
3 A.M.
MIDNIGHT
SUNSET
NOON
MELBOURNE
KING ISLAND
E.N.E.
50 ML S.W OTWAY
POSITION GIVEN
IN EVIDENCE

| 50 | 0 | 50 | 100 | 150 | 200 |

NAUTICAL MILES

EPILOGUE

34
SEA CHANGE

There have been sequels to the stories of both the *Schomberg* and the *Loch Ard*. Even before 1870 rumours began to circulate on the South Island of New Zealand that the remains of a wooden ship lay not far from the mouth of Tauperikaka Creek, a wild, remote spot, difficult of access, well south on the west coast. In 1871 the reports were investigated and a piece of wreckage over twenty feet long by twelve feet wide was brought out for examination. The party that had gone in reported that the ship had been a very large one. The section brought out aroused great interest because of its unusual construction: the wood was in layers on the diagonal principle; also, trenails had been used. Four years later an even larger section was brought out by sea and the belief was expressed that the ship could be none other than the *Schomberg*, or, at any rate, a large part of her. To corroborate the theory a piece was sent to Halls of Aberdeen. They identified it as having come from the ship they had launched with such pride in 1855.

It was extraordinary that such a large part of the *Schomberg* should have drifted so far—an estimated fifteen hundred miles. Was anything left in the waters where she had sunk? Certainly local fishermen had seen rails marked "Krupp" against the reef where she had struck; also the ship's bell had been retrieved very early and was hung first at St John's Presbyterian church in Warrnambool and later at the Presbyterian church at the settlement of Woodford, north of Warrnambool, but was returned. A second bell—a mess bell—was in the hands of the Warrnambool Public Library. But the general opinion seemed to be that the hull of the ship itself was buried under sand off the reef. Perhaps this belief persisted because few local people knew of the New Zealand reports, even though they appeared again in 1920. In any case, the wreck did not excite prolonged search, as the *Loch Ard* was to do, perhaps because her cargo was relatively mundane and probably irretrievable. So serious search around Peterborough for the *Schomberg* lagged for a hundred and eighteen years.

In the meantime there were many searches for the *Loch Ard*. Carrying copper and lead and much else of value, she was worth seeking, despite the dangers of the seas around the gorge. But the more the searches went on, the more conflicting did opinion become as to the wreck's whereabouts. Some searchers believed it to be within the gorge—a not altogether unreasonable conclusion, since many oddments of wreckage were found there, and during the First World War Hugh Gibson's young nephew uncovered a piano on the gorge beach.

The more methodical searchers went to the original records and to the elderly local people who had seen the "solitary spar a few feet out of the water", as the *Argus* had described it. The spar soon disappeared and gradually the years devoured all those who had seen it: Tom Pearce, the Gibsons, the Shields, George Ford, Charles McGillivray, Constable Graham, all the unidentified local people whose children's children were to treasure relics picked up in those days. Last of all, William Till died at the age of ninety-six in 1956. Then there was no one left who had seen the spar, or spoken to Tom Pearce.

Those who were convinced in the pre-1939 years that the wreckage lay against Mutton Bird Island had scant hope of proving their point, since there was little possibility of diving in the area without deep-sea equipment. After the Second World War aqualungs came into general use and new impetus was lent the search, but for twenty more years there was still no success.

In September 1964 a *Warrnambool Standard* skindiving correspondent reported that "the area in which the *Loch Ard* is reputed to have met her end has been combed by these underwater explorers in depths ranging from 30 to 100 feet, but with little result". By that time at least one group had been involved in the search for five years. Its members were local men: Stan McPhee and George Battarbee of Warrnambool, Cliff Sharp of Port Campbell, and Don Baird of Princetown. Because the repeated hiring of boats became a matter of considerable expense to them, Baird spent two years building one.

In 1967 the group finally achieved success. News of their find was not released to the press for two more years. The *Warrnambool Standard* of 4th February 1969 related what had happened: "It was on February 5th, 1967, that McPhee and Battarbee, working from Baird's boat, made the first sighting of the wreck. Stan McPhee made the first dive that day and had been under for 55 minutes. . . . He had only five minutes' supply left when he sighted two symmetrical shapes, about twenty feet below." McPhee later returned to the spot and there, between sixty and seventy feet down, he found her. The two sections of the hull were well apart, lying on either side of the reef that had claimed her, the bow looking like a reef itself. The wooden top deck that had parted from the iron hull had long since rotted away, but large pieces of limestone dislodged from the cliffs by the yard-arm could still be seen about the wreckage. Two or three cowbells lay in the sand near by. There were rents in the hull large enough to admit a man. On a later dive McPhee entered by one of these and found tumbled casks and cargo that had lain nearly ninety years in that pale-green, swaying world.

McPhee and his companions were aware that the *Loch Ard* had carried a cargo of considerable value. They had themselves seen pigs of lead, marked "Pontifex & Wood, London", each over a hundred pounds in weight, and bolts of copper over thirty pounds. Salvaging such items presented problems enough, but a greater problem lay in the legal ramifications of the case. Who, after all, owned the wreck?

McPhee's party were aware that their activities over the wreck site had been observed from the cliff-tops and that the question of ownership should be settled quickly to avoid illegal intrusions. McPhee himself had written within a week of their find to the Victorian Receiver of Wreck, in the Department of Shipping and Transport, describing the location of the *Loch Ard* and itemizing the limited relics that he and his party had recovered.

The lure of such a find drew others to the site. There came then into the search a party of abalone fishermen known about the straits as "the Tassie boys". Skilful seamen and divers, accustomed to a life of risk, they sound like descendants of the Straitsmen. They began diving on the *Loch Ard* and blasting her hull for easier removal of cargo. It was this intrusion that led to announcement in the *Warrnambool Standard* of the discovery two years after McPhee's party had made their successful dive. Stories began appearing in local papers: "A Warrnambool resident said yeaterday that some time ago he had seen several men loading lead ingots onto a truck near the mouth of the Sherbrooke River. The lead had apparently been cached in a sandy bay near the mouth of the river. Thousands of dollars worth of lead and copper is reported to have been recovered from the wreck and it is understood much of it has been sold."

In the Melbourne *Herald* the *Loch Ard* began to rate headlines many times larger than those that had announced her end. Before long there were claimants to the wreck. Two descendants of the Miller partner of Howarth, Miller and Matthews laid claim to the ship their great-uncle had been forced to give up ninety-one years before.

At this point the Australian Government took action. It was found that much of the salvaged cargo had been sold; that over two hundred pigs of lead had been hidden on a farm near Cobden. A round-up of cargo was made by Commonwealth and State police. The Receiver of Wreck posted a notice at the Geelong Customs House listing "wreck" of which he had already taken possession.

A case was brought against two of the "Tassie boys" for "failure to declare possession of wreck" and "attempt to mislead". The defendants did not appear when the case came up at Camperdown in December 1969. By this time they had vanished over the strait—it was believed to King Island. They were each fined $50 with costs of $62.50—small enough sums compared with their probable profits.

On Boxing Day 1972 there was a first hint of a *Schomberg* find. A Timboon man, Ron Cashmore, was fishing in Newfield Bay about half a mile east of the Schomberg Reef. His anchor snagged. When he dived on it he found it to be caught in the barnacled hull of a large ship.

Stan McPhee, as redoubtable a man in his conflicts with the sea as the vanished masters themselves, went to the spot in the boat of another Warrnambool diver, John Laidlaw. On 22nd August 1973 they re-located Cashmore's find thirty feet down. It was undoubtedly the *Schomberg*. It lay in the area where tradition had it that a towline broke when an attempt was made to tow the ship off the reef, stern first. But McPhee saw that the bows section of the wreck was missing. The stern was hard against a reef, suggesting the impact which years before had caused the towline to break. Thus it would appear that the bows drifted, nautilus-like, to New Zealand. A comparison was made during 1976 of timbers from the New Zealand find and timbers from the remains of the hull at Peterborough. They proved to be from the same ship. McPhee and Laidlaw went on to salvage brass rudder fittings— the five gudgeons and five pinels that allowed the rudder to pivot in answer to the helm. Each pair was about six feet long, cast in brass four inches thick and sixteen inches wide—dimensions that give some idea of the size of the ship. The five sets weighed 1200 pounds.

On New Year's Day 1976 there was a further discovery at the site. Two Warrnambool divers recovered an unexpected relic from the *Schomberg*'s hull: a cannon, six feet long with a bore of four inches. In the years when attacks by pirates were common in eastern seas, it was not unusual for large passenger ships to be equipped with armament. Fittingly, the relic was taken to the Flagstaff Hill Maritime Village at Warrnambool.

Later in 1976 legislation was introduced to protect historic ship-wrecks. Under the Commonwealth Historic Shipwrecks Act it is an offence to interfere with or remove relics from declared wrecks. The *Loch Ard* is one such wreck, the *Schomberg* another.

Divers may study them and marvel over the time capsules they have become, but they can no longer legally remove anything from them.

35
SAFETY

Although no further passenger-carrying ships were wrecked on the Otway coast after the loss of the *Loch Ard*, a toll was still exacted among cargo ships: *Eric the Red*, *Edinburgh Castle*, *Fiji*, *Newfield*, *Falls of Halladale*. The bones of them lie between Peterborough and Cape Otway. In shops and homes thereabouts one may see photographs taken from the shore of doomed ships, startlingly close in, so that in one the sailors may be plainly seen clinging to the bowsprit across boiling surf.

The toll only ended when the era of sail ended and mariners no longer faced the threat of being pinned to a lee shore. Even by the time the *Loch Ard* was lost, the public could view the wreck and its aftermath secure in the knowledge that if they travelled by sea they could go now by steam. In 1869 the Suez Canal had been opened; in 1879, the year after the wreck of the *Loch Ard*, the 5400-ton auxiliary steamship *Orient* entered the Australian run as the name ship of her line. By 1882 the total tonnage of steamships on the British register passed that of sail. Ironically, many a splendid sailing ship became a coal hulk for the new lords of the sea.

No words could better express the feelings of many of the outgoing sailing-ship men than those of Captain Horn, who for almost twenty-six years had commanded the *Loch Garry*:

This is a utilitarian age and the race is now all for the mighty dollar. The clippers of the palmy days of ocean sailing have gone never to return; the beautiful things of life, which fired the ambition and disciplined the will of our forefathers, have given place to a class of vessel which is oppressed in every way by the dire necessity for rigid economy in every department and it is now almost impossible to rival the deeds, which, even now, call forth the utmost enthusiasm.

After sixty-two years at sea, Captain Horn must be allowed his splendid words, but it is to be remembered that the greatest feats of the clippers were in pursuit of gold and that many a fortune was made by shipowners in a heartless gamble with passengers' lives.

Wind power had been free, but like fire, it was a fearful master. The fact that steamships did not have to suffer the dictates of the wind was the biggest step towards safety in the confined Otway–Wickham entrance to Bass Strait.

As the passenger-carrying days of sail in the strait drew to a close, so too did the days of Henry Bayles Ford at Cape Otway. In November 1878 he applied again to the Victorian Government for permission to retire on superannuation. "I pray [my application] may be granted as both myself and Mrs Ford's health is fast breaking up." They were withdrawn in January 1879 after thirty years of the highest public service. Shortly afterwards it was ruled that keepers would not be required to serve at remote lighthouses for periods exceeding two years.

In 1891 the original apparatus that had served Ford for so many years at Otway was replaced by a revolving lens, "of the First Order" and kerosene replaced oil. Shortly before the First World War the Commonwealth of Australia prepared to take over many lighthouses from the States. Commander C. R. W. Brewis, R.N., carried out a large-scale survey of existing lights. In 1913 he classified Cape Otway as "an important landfall light", but when he came to consider Cape Wickham he wrote: "As reefs extend for a distance of $4\frac{1}{2}$ miles to seaward, the tides being very treacherous, setting strongly towards King Island . . . vessels should give this locality a wide berth and not be encouraged to approach within signalling distance." As a result of his report, the signalling station was closed. Five years later Wickham itself became an unmanned, automatic light.

Although the coming of steam was the greatest single factor bringing safety to the western entrance of Bass Strait—as it did to many another stretch of dangerous water—full security was not assured until the Second World War. In 1939 electric power was brought to Otway and a radio beacon installed there. Two years later a similar beacon was installed at Cape Wickham. Used in conjunction, these two beacons enabled approaching ships to fix their position regardless of weather.

But with the advent of satellite navigation even this safeguard became outmoded. Ships now knew their position with such accuracy that, in 1992, the radio beacons were closed down. In 1994 Cape Otway's sandstone tower, built 146 years earlier, was itself decommissioned and replaced with a solar-powered light installed on glass reinforced plastic. The closing of the old lighthouse was seen by thousands of Victorians as the closing of a significant era in Australia's history. On the day preceding its last night of operation over 3000 people visited it; a thousand stayed on, including families of past keepers, to see it light up for the last time. Speeches were amplified and a piper, spot-lighted on the lighthouse balcony, played a lament. It was an occasion redolent of the era of sail.

Waves still pound the Schomberg Reef and Mutton Bird Island; the hulls that were the pride of Captain Forbes and Captain Gibb still hold some of their secrets. Unless the Cremona violin was washed ashore in its brass case and was taken to one of the district's homes, it must be presumed lost among the wreckage of the *Loch Ard* for ever. But in 1975 the Minton peacock was purchased for the Warrnambool Maritime Village for public display. For seventy-seven years it had remained in possession of the Miller family—the Miller of the salvage firm Howarth, Miller and Matthews. On 1st June 1935, the fifty-seventh anniversary of the wreck, it was displayed at the Melbourne Museum. Advertised as a "wonderful piece of ceramic art ... valued at £2000", it was purchased by another Melbourne family and remained with them until purchased by the Maritime Village for $4500.

Another of the five peacocks made by Mintons is displayed at the Peacock Hotel in the Derbyshire village of Rowsley. This is also claimed to have come from the wreck of the *Loch Ard*. It is highly improbable that Mintons would have risked sending two exhibits of such value on the one ship and less likely that, if they had, both would have been washed ashore. If by some extraordinary chance this had happened, newspaper men would have been quick to report it.

Where I. Keith McIntyre delivered his short address from the words, "And the sea gave up the dead which were in it", there has accumulated a group of pioneer graves, but it is the Carmichael stone that draws people of later generations. The mood of its inscription is at one with the coast and the sea.

Glenample lay derelict and largely neglected. The Melbourne architect, Allan Willingham, an authority on the stone houses of the Western District of Victoria, fortunately preserved detailed plans of the homestead as it had been in Hugh Gibson's day, always hoping that restoration would prove possible. In 1980 its owner agreed to a ninety-nine year lease of the homestead and its immediate surroundings to the State Government; in 1988–89 Allan Willingham's long perserverance was rewarded: the Ministry of Conservation, Forests and Lands funded large-scale restoration. Thus was begun a repository, open to the public, of *Loch Ard* memorabilia, relics and pictures; memorabilia, too, of the Gibson family and those associated with them—a fitting role for a home that is so much part of Victoria's heritage.

Appendix 1

Passenger List of the *Schomberg*

These names are drawn from the Melbourne *Argus*. The issue of 29th December 1855 listed thirty-one first class passengers or family groups. The issue of 31st December listed all other classes. Neither list was in alphabetical order. Since the following list has been arranged alphabetically, it brings together passengers of the same name. It cannot be assumed that such passengers are of the same family. It would appear from the *Argus* lists that family groups are specified as such.

Aarons, Louis
Aarons, Mary M.
Abella, W.
Abbott, Jos., wife & two
  daughters
Adams, Edw.
Allen, Joseph G.
Angore, John & Thomas
Annear, Sam
Ash, Martin
Ashe, Henry
Azavedo, Isaac

Bach, S., wife & two children
Bedford, John
Best, Alfred
Black, Andrew
Black, John
Blane, Robert
Boggs, George
Boland, Ann
Bowes, Henry

Brunner, Thomas
Bryans, Christopher
Buesnel, —
Buesnel, Miss
Buesnel, Frances
Buesnel, Patrick
Buesnel, Ph. H.
Bulfin, Mr

Caircross, George
Callan, James
Cameron, Angus & Alexander
Campbell, Wm.
Carpenter, Mr
Carr, James
Carr, John
Casey, Robert & Henry
Casey, William
Casper, Mary & four children
Charles, Joseph
Charnock & wife
Chislett, Jacob

Clark, Charlotte
Clark, Elizabeth
Clarke, Dr Jonathan
Clifford, A.
Clifford, A. C.
Coles, Thomas
Connolly, James
Consterdine, Benjamin
Corelter, Henry J.
Cotton, James & Hugh
Coughan, Thomas
Cowie, James, lady & family
Craig, John
Crebban, Richard & wife
Crough, Andrew
Crowley, John

D'Angri, Natale
Daniel, Mr
Davies, William
Dempster, David
Devery, Thomas
Dineen, Michael & William
Dixon, Thos. H.
Donnellan, James
Drury, Frank
Dunyer, Mr

Edwards, Matilda
Ellerton, John

Featherley, Benjamin, wife &
    three children
Featherly, George, wife & two
    children
Fenn, Charles
Foster, James
Fraser, James

Galletti, Anthony
Gedkin, Mr
Gleeson, William

Goffney, Adelia
Gordon, James
Green, Margaret & three
    children
Grieve, James
Griffin, James
Griffin, John
Grunthall, Louis

Hadley, Mrs & three children
Hamilton, George
Hammer, Joseph
Harrington, Ellen
Harrison, Harry R.
Harrison, W.
Hart, Fanny
Hartwell, John
Hawker, George C., wife,
    family & servants
Heath, Samuel
Henderson, George, wife &
    two children
Hennessy, C. & John
Heyan, Mary
Hinchard, Arthur
Hodgson, Henry & wife
Hogan, Pat
Hogarth, Daniel
Hogarty, William & wife
Holgate, Enoch
Hopkins, James, John &
    Edward
Houghan, Patrick
Humphrey, Mr & wife

Isaacs, Robert M., lady, family
    & servants

Johnson, Thos
Johnson, William
Jones, Elizabeth
Joynt, Charles

Kannard, James
Kebsar, George
Kelson, Isaac & lady
Kemble, Robert
Kenneen, Lawrence
Kinane, Michael
Knapman, George
Knowles, Henry

Lace, John & Ann
Lamoran, Duncan & Angus
Lamoran, Janet
Landon, J. C. C.
Lassidy, William & Thomas
Lazarus, Sanloc
Lee, Margaret
Leighton, David (sen.) &
  David (jun.)
Lewis, John
Lewis, Mary E. & seven
  children
Long, William
Lorhihan, Pat

Magee, Wm.
Magrath, James
Maher, Thomas
Mainland, Hugh
Marshmill, Thomas
Martin, Louisa & four children
Mathieson, Alexr.
Moor, James B.
Morris, Mr, wife & three
  children
Millar, John F.
Murray, James
Myers, Mary & one child

M'Avory, Patrick
Mackintosh, William
M'Cormack, Patrick
Macdonnell, H.

M'Gemskin & wife
M'Ilwraith, George
M'Ilwraith, Hugh

Nixon, Julia

Oates, Nicholas
O'Farrell, Wm. R.
O'Neill, William
Ongey, John D.

Palmer, Angelo C.
Palmer, Ann J. & five children
Panton, John
Patey, William
Patton, Andrew
Paul, James, wife & three
  children
Pearson, John
Pearson, William
Padler, Edwin
Perez, Julia
Pinch, John E.
Pratt, Charles
Purlis, W. G.

Ray, Francis
Read, John
Redhead, Garvil
Redhead, John
Reed, Wm.
Roberts, Mrs & child
Robertson, Jane
Robson, James
Rolleston, James
Ross, Rev. William, lady &
  servant
Russell, Arthur
Ryan, Michael
Ryan, Patrick & wife
Ryan, Pat
Ryan, Thomas & Pat

Sands, Prof. J. C., lady & child
Sellors, Thos. & wife
Sherwood, Edward
Smeaton, John & Margaret
Smith, Eleanor
Smith, James S.
Smith, John
Smith, William
Snow, David
Solomon, Lewis
Solomon, Mrs
Stephens, Elizabeth
Stewart, Peter
Stockdall, Alexander
Sutton, Emma & three children

Taylor, Joseph
Templeman, George
Templeman, Henry
Tretheway, William
Trethowan, Sarah A.
Turnbull, William
Turner, Austin T.

Unmack, Carl
Upton, William & Christopher

Vaff, Wm.

Walker, Mrs
Walker, Miss
Walker, John
Walker, Miss Sarah
Watts, Mr, Mrs & Miss
Welsh, Thomas
Weston, Julia
Wharton, George
Whatterton, B.
Whelan, Adam
White, Miss
White & wife
Wilkie, Joseph
Wilkinson, Thomas, wife & three children
Williams, E. P.
Williams, Henry M.
Wilson, James
Wright, Thomas & wife

Note: This list totals 320, excluding unspecified family and servant numbers of the passengers Cowie, Hawker, and Isaacs. On departure, 351 sailed.

Appendix 2

The Angove Diary

Several years after this book first appeared the shipboard diary of a *Schomberg* passenger, Thomas Angove, was passed to the author. Angove's name is incorrectly shown on the passenger list published in the Melbourne *Argus* as "Angore".

Extracts from the diary throw much light on the voyage and on the *Schomberg*'s flamboyant master. Like most people of the time, Angove was awed by the *Schomberg*'s spread of canvas:

We have no less than 33 sails spread on different masts. There is not a ship afloat that carries so much canvas. The main yard is 110 feet long, the mainsail about 100 feet in length.

But in the doldrums their array of sails was of little use to them; they were so becalmed that the captain of another becalmed ship came over for dinner with Forbes. The meal over, the *Schomberg*'s German band provided dance music for the first class passengers. In Angove's view

—this would have been acceptable enough if they had knocked off at a reasonable hour; but not so. They kept jigging away all night before the stranger returned to his ship. Nor did it end there. A party with Captain Forbes at its head accompanied the seagoing visitor to his ship and stayed for some considerable time.

During this long period of jollity a breeze had sprung up, but Forbes took no advantage of it. Extraordinary behaviour for a man aiming for a fast passage!

From his diary it seems likely that Angove was one of the passengers quoted in the Melbourne press following the protest meeting there, for he writes of two incidents mentioned at the meeting. Off South America Forbes ordered his helmsman to sail close to a passing ship:

(Our) fore stunsail boom took away her colours as clean as a whistle. She was a Yankee ship and no doubt her captain felt indignant at the *Schomberg*'s insolence.

The second incident occurred in latitude 50 degrees south where Forbes twice ran close to large icebergs to allow passengers to look at them. According to Angove ''he ran the vessel so close (to one) that the keel must have gone over portion of it.''

The reader can only assume that Forbes was by then exasperated that he had no hope of setting another record; exasperation was to be part of his undoing.

Appendix 3

Numbers Brought to Australia by Captain Forbes

In making out ships' papers before a voyage commenced, it was the practice to show emigrants in groupings of English, Scotch, Irish, and Other Countries. Welsh emigrants were included with those from England. The following lists cover Captain Forbes's four famous voyages to Melbourne. On none of these voyages were any passengers shown as other than English, Scotch, or Irish, although, by name, several would appear to have been of European origin. In the table for the *Schomberg* the further subdivision showing destinations is included. Among the illustrations appears a photo-copy of the Melbourne and Geelong sheet, bearing Captain Forbes's signature. From this it will be seen that the number of "statute passengers" was derived by assessing a child as numerically less than one adult.

MARCO POLO
Arrived 20.9.1852

	English	*Scotch*	*Irish*	*Total*
Adults	37	422	144	603
Children Between 14 & 1	16	218	59	293
Infants	2	21	11	34
		Total on Departure		930

MARCO POLO
Arrived 12.3.1853

	English	*Scotch*	*Irish*	*Total*
Adults	527	—	31	558
Children Between 14 & 1	38	—	3	41
Infants	6	—	1	7
		Total on Departure		606

LIGHTNING
Arrived 13.5.1854

	English	Scotch	Irish	Total
Adults	390	—	4	394
Children Between 14 & 1	45	—	—	45
Infants	13	—	—	13
			Total on Departure	452

SCHOMBERG
Wrecked 26.12.1855

Passengers to Sydney

	English	Scotch	Irish	Total
Adults	24	—	5	29
Children Between 14 & 1	5	—	4	9
Infants	—	—	1	1
				39

Passengers to Adelaide

	English	Scotch	Irish	Total
Adults	8	—	4	12
Children Between 14 & 1	5	—	4	9
Infants	2	—	1	3
				24

Passengers to Melbourne & Geelong

	English	Scotch	Irish	Total
Adults	157	15	68	240
Children Between 14 & 1	32	4	3	39
Infants	8	1	—	9
				288
			Total on Departure	351

Appendix 4

The Loch Ships

Loch Ard built 1873, wrecked 1878 near Port Campbell with loss of 52 lives.

Loch Awe built 1869, sold to Norwegian owners 1912, sunk by German submarine during First World War.

Loch Broom built 1885, sold to Norwegian owners 1912, sunk by German submarine 1917.

Loch Carron built 1885, collided with *Inverskip* 1904, resulting in £30,000 damages against Loch Line; sold to Norwegian owners 1912, sunk in collision at sea 1915.

Loch Earn built 1869, collided with *Ville de Havre* in mid-Atlantic 1873. Both ships lost with 226 lives.

Loch Etive built 1877 (Joseph Conrad one of her officers); sold to French owners 1911; ultimately became a coal hulk.

Loch Fyne built 1876, not seen after leaving New Zealand for England 1883.

Loch Garry built 1875, sold to Italian owners and broken up 1911.

Loch Katrine built 1869, sold to Australian owners 1910 and used as coastal collier; ended her days as a coal hulk in Rabaul Harbour.

Loch Laggan built 1872 (formerly *America*), disappeared at sea 1878.

Loch Leven built 1870, wrecked King Island 1871 soon after departure from Geelong.

Loch Lomond built 1870, lost en route Newcastle, N.S.W., to Lyttelton, New Zealand, 1908.

Loch Long built 1876, not sighted after leaving Melbourne for New Caledonia 1903, presumed all hands lost when wreckage picked up on Chatham Islands.

Loch Maree built 1873, last seen leaving Bass Strait west-bound 1881.

Loch Moidart built 1881, wrecked on Dutch coast 1890.

Loch Ness built 1869, converted into a coal hulk 1910, towed to sea and sunk by gunfire 1926.

Loch Nevis built 1894 (last vessel built for the Loch Line), seriously damaged by fire 1900, sold to German owners, again damaged by fire; a hulk till converted to steam in 1919 by Argentina; destroyed by fire off Patagonian coast 1922.

Loch Rannoch built 1869, sold to Norwegian owners 1907, resold to German owners in 1910 and broken up.

Loch Ryan built 1877, purchased by Australian Commonwealth Line and renamed *John Murray*, wrecked Maldon Island 1918.

Loch Shiel built 1877, wrecked on Thorne Rocks, Milford Haven, 1901.

Loch Sloy built 1877, wrecked Kangaroo Island 1889, only four survivors.

Loch Sunart built 1878, wrecked 1879 off coast of Ireland.

Loch Tay built 1869, sold to Huddart Parker for a coal hulk at Port Adelaide 1910, broken up 1958.

Loch Torridon built 1881, torpedoed in English Channel 1915.

Loch Vennachar built 1875, wrecked Kangaroo Island 1905 with all hands.

Note: The New Zealand company of James Sproat also ran a line of "Loch" Ships for several years: *Loch Cree, Loch Dee, Loch Doon, Loch Fleet, Loch Ken, Loch Trool, Loch Urr*. These ships were considerably smaller than the Aitken, Lilburn ships listed above.

Appendix 5

Voyages of the *Loch Ard*

	Date Voyage Began	Port Voyage Began	Date Voyage Ended	Port Voyage Ended	Master	Ports of Call
1.	4/12/73	Glasgow	30/12/73	Greenock	F. J. Green	Voyage to Australia & N.Z. intended, but put back for repairs.
2.	6/1/74	Greenock	11/2/75	London	W. Robertson	Melbourne.
3.	8/4/75	London	18/2/76	London	W. Robertson	Melbourne.
4.	18/4/76	London	18/12/76	London	C. Buchanan	Calcutta.
5.	7/2/77	Glasgow	1/1/78	London	J. Mackay	Melbourne.
7.	3/3/78	London	1/6/78	Vessel lost Curdie's Inlet, Australia	George Gibb	None recorded.

Note: In providing this information the Board of Trade's General Register and Record Office of Shipping and Seamen has remarked: "The information above has been extracted from lists of the Crew. Only in respect of the first voyage (1.) is the Official Log Book available. The ports of call details are limited to ports at which the Shipping Master or similar officer has endorsed the documents and may not necessarily represent all ports of call."

Appendix 6

Manifest of the *Loch Ard*

TOTAL DECLARED VALUE: £53,700

5671 pieces and packages of softgoods, 17 packages of fancy goods:

Plain cottons £657
Woollens & worsted £175
Goods £94
Sewing thread £46
Apparel £715
Straw hats £36
Wrought leather £180
Table baize £26
Paper 481 cwt (64 bales)
Upholstery £1862
Preserved fish £20
Isinglass & gelatine 31 lb.
Arrowroot 10 cwt
Raisins 172 cwt
White salt 50 tons
Candles 87 cwt
Liquorice juice 30 cwt
Confectionery 15 cases
Canary seed 29 cwt
Camphor £39
Perfumery £9
Safety fuse £464
Agric. & garden seed £416
Apothecaries' ware £570
Tin hardware & cutlery £7530
Furniture 56 packages
Pianos £733

Iron bedsteads £321
Lines & twines £490
Tobacconists' ware & tobacco 164 packages (cigars 270 lb., snuff 212 lb., tobacco 27,155 lb., clay pipes £100)
Oils & paints 1028 packs (linseed oil 10,328 gal., paint and colors £2446.)
Glue 10 cwt
Cod oil 539 gal.
Sawn wood (844 deals 60 loads)
Colored cottons £107
Linen in bales £95
Millinery £74
Haberdashery £854
Carpets & rugs £415
Felt hats & caps £125
Saddlery £22 (2 packs)
Vestas 472 cases
Printed cottons £252
W'proof india rubber
Hosiery £336
Umbrellas £11
Counterpanes £95
Dressed leather £210
Floor cloth £786

Books £371 (1 case)

Stationery £381 (105 packages)

Paper & Papier mache goods £993

Pepper & spices 20 cwt; split peas 31 cwt

Crystals 36 tons

Soap 42 cwt

Figs 52 cwt; dates 20 cwt, ginger 95 cwt

Coffee 31 cwt, carroway seed 47 cwt

Sulphur 200 cwt (200 barrels)

Alum 40 cwt; tartaric acid 10 cwt

Miscellaneous 26 cases (92 packages)

Corks £11

Clocks and Watches £25

Printing material £118

Kero & naptha 175 gal. (27 drums)

Pitch & tar, 4 barrels 35 drums

Rape oil 5370 gal.

Olive oil bulk 52 gal.

Glass (604 cases):

Plate glass (4 cases)

Foreign window glass (610 cases)

China & earthenware £355

Marble £400

Flint glass £479

Window glass £24

Glass bottles £61

Brandy bulk 8827 gal.

Brandy case 1920 gal.

British spirits in bulk 3391 gal.

British spirits case 95 gal.

White wine 868 gal.

Beer in glass 141 gal.

Foreign & salad oil 755 gal.

Rum 125 gal.

Cordials 82 gal.

Geneva 13,600 gal.

Perfumed spirit 1 gal.

Red wine 3400 gal.

Assorted oils in stone £1958

Cement 400 barrels (1000 casks)

Agric. implements £607 (6 bundles shovels, 29 chaff cutters, 61 anvils)

Rails & Gen. machinery £4049: 11 machines; 34 pair mail axle arms; 4 pieces of castings; Iron rails 30 tons (1448 rails); iron tanks £6

Bar and Rod iron 102 tons ⎤ 176 bundles & 102 single tubes; 43
Hoop iron 3 tons ⎬ plates, 4631 bars & 1283 bundles of
Plate iron 3 tons ⎦ iron

Chain & anchor £8 (36 anchors)
Lead shot 22 tons (2 casks)
Wire and rope 2 tons
78 camp ovens & covers
Firearms £173
Nails 110 kegs.
Fittings gas (4 cases)
165 slate slabs

Sheet iron 13 tons (22 bundles)
Galv. iron 128 tons (75 cases)
Steel 9 tons (152 cases-bundles)
Zinc 12 tons
Copper 33 plates, 53 bolts
Rivets 4 casks
Pig lead 50 tons (994 pig & 37 rolls)

Appendix 7

By the 1970s there was growing realization that the wreck of the *Loch Ard* approximated the end of the settlement of Victoria by immigrants under sail. In 1978 the Victorian Government observed the centenary not only of the wreck, but of the long era of which it symbolised the end. At Easter and in the June of that year numerous commemorative events were held to remind the public of the great part sailing ships had played in pioneering the State. The most memorable was the linking on Easter Monday of Cape Otway and King Island by radio so that crowds at both ends could hear their local school children recounting the deeds of ships' masters, lighthouse keepers and explorers. Each child prefixed the alternating readings with, 'I am the voice of ——' — the voice of Eva Carmichael, of Henry Bayles Ford, of Edward Spong, of Superintendent La Trobe.

By that Easter, Victorian scuba divers had completed the dangerous task of raising of one the *Loch Ard's* anchors. It was brought by them into Port Campbell before large Easter Monday crowds, ultimately to be placed at the entrance to the National Parks Information Centre there.

Far off in London the Agent General for Victoria unveiled a plaque at Gravesend, the departure place of the *Loch Ard* on her last voyage. All of the June events in Victoria related specifically to the *Loch Ard*. On Saturday 2nd, in gales and driving rain, nearly 2000 people gathered before dawn in the shelter of the Loch Ard Gorge. There, with the house flag of Aitken, Lilburn flying, a commemorative service was held by the light of several bonfires. A piper played a lament and an address was given, ending with the words:

The passengers who were lost here in June 1878 were the last of many hundreds of emigrant passengers who perished at the western entrance to Bass Strait during the era of sail, perished either on this shore or — in greater numbers — on King Island. In our company this morning are descendants of several of those associated with the wreck of the *Loch Ard*. With them we have gathered not only to recall the great courage and endurance shown here where we stand, but to remember also those hundreds of thousands of our forbears who reached these shores safely after long and arduous passages by sail, and lived to found homes and families in the new land. All honour to the memory of those who lived and those who died.

When daylight came, the local pony club riders relayed to Camperdown post office a replica of Hugh Gibson's telegram telling the outside world of the *Loch Ard* disaster — a re-enactment of George Ford's epic ride. That night a capacity crowd attended a 'Grand Tom Pearce Ball' in Timboon at which local people in period costume danced a set to the lively music of the 'Tom Pearce Schottische'.

These celebrations gave great impetus to tourism along what has become known as "the Shipwreck Coast" and led to further commemorative events over the years. At one of these a descendant of Captain Forbes, Mr. Peter Magee, of Brisbane, was able to display lengths of deep navy blue French brocade, believed to have been curtains from the *Schomberg*. These had been given by Forbes to his half-sister, Isabella Nicol. Isabella had come out to Melbourne with Forbes in the *Lightning* at the age of eighteen. Travelling for the benefit of her health, she fell in love with a passenger, Blakiston Robinson; they were married in Melbourne, Forbes giving her away. It is believed that Forbes stayed with the Robinsons during the *Schomberg* enquiries and gave the lengths of material to them at this time.

Commemorative events along the coast continue. One can well imagine that they would surprise such men as Tom Pearce, Henry Bayles Ford and Hugh Gibson. Like so many other men and women of their time, they were simply doing what they saw as their duty.

INDEX